SHERLOCK HOLMES AND THE SIGN OF FOUR

A Play in Two Acts
Based on the stories by Arthur Conan Doyle

Eric J. McAnallen

Copyright © 2013 Eric J. McAnallen

All rights reserved.

ISBN-13: 978-1500613686
ISBN-10: 1500613681

Professionals and amateurs are hereby warned that this work is subject to a royalty. Royalty must be paid every time a play is performed whether or not it is presented for profit and whether or not admission is charged. A play is performed any time it is acted before an audience. All rights to this work of any kind including but not limited to professional and amateur stage performing rights are controlled exclusively by the author, Eric J. McAnallen.

This work is fully protected by copyright. No part of this work may be reproduced, stored in a retrieval system, or transmitted in any form or by any means, electronic, mechanical, photocopying, recording or otherwise, without permission of the author. Copying (by any means) or performing a copyrighted work without permission constitutes an infringement of copyright.

All organizations receiving permission to produce this work agree to give the author credit in any and all advertisement and publicity relating to the production. The author billing must appear below the title and be at least 50% as large as the title of the Work.

There shall be no deletions, alterations, or changes of any kind made to the work, including changing of character gender, the cutting of dialogue, or the alteration of objectionable language unless directed authorized by the author. The title of the play shall not be altered.

The right of performance is not transferable and is strictly forbidden in cases where scripts are borrowed or purchased second-hand from a third party. All rights, including but not limited to professional and amateur stage performing, recitation, lecturing, public reading, television, radio, motion picture, video or sound taping, internet streaming or other forms of broadcast as technology progresses, and the rights of translation into foreign languages, are strictly reserved.

COPYING OR REPRODUCING ALL OR ANY PART OF THIS BOOK IN ANY MANNER IS STRICTLY FORBIDDEN BY LAW. One copy for each speaking role must be purchased for production purposes. Single copies of scripts are sold for personal reading or production consideration only.

To obtain production rights or to inquire about alterations, contact the author.

Eric J. McAnallen
P.O. Box 21 · Ellwood City, PA 16117
http://www.capnmac.com · inquires@capnmac.com
(724) 201-9694

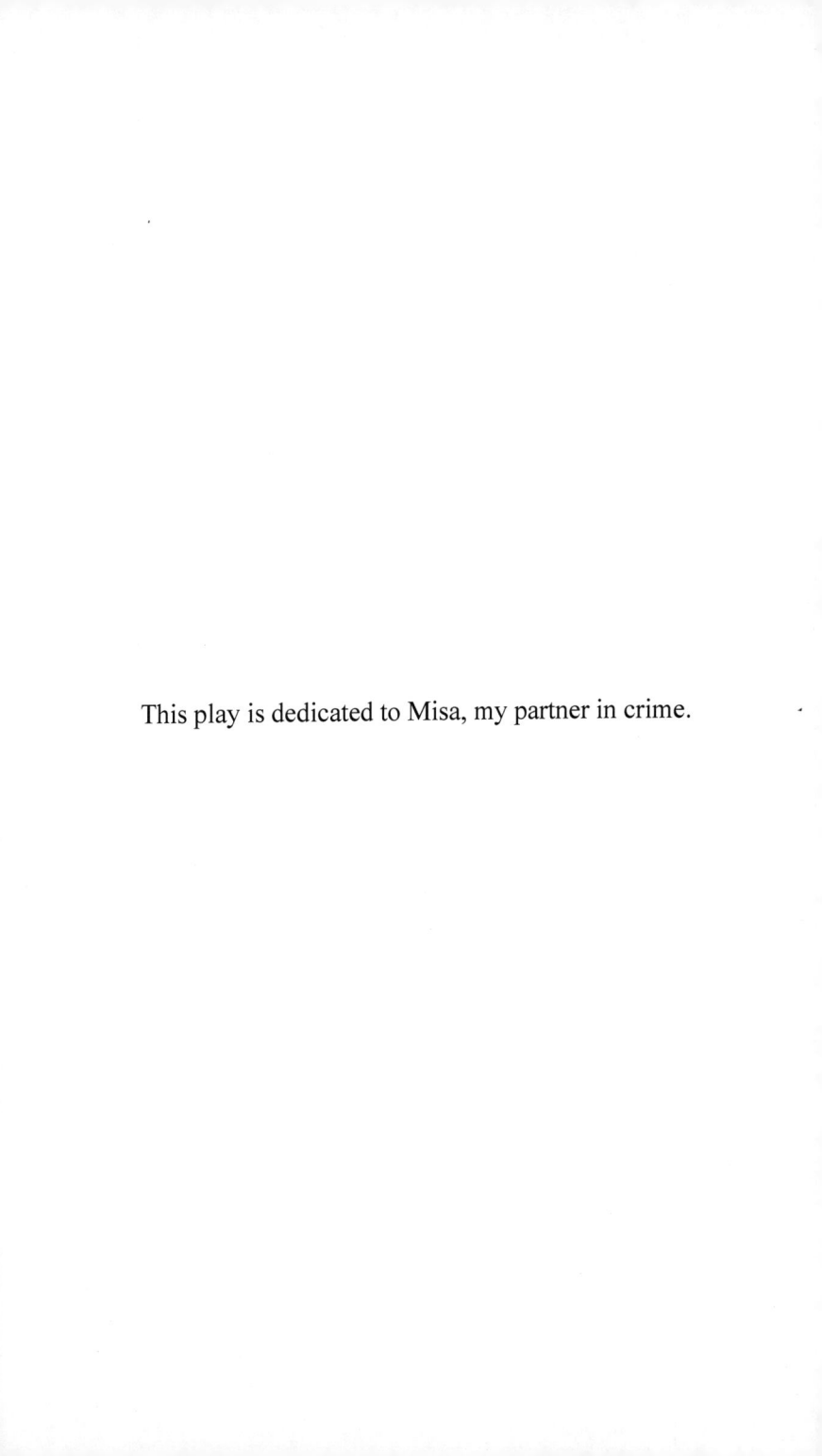

This play is dedicated to Misa, my partner in crime.

Synopsis

Dr. John Watson, wounded and fresh off the front lines in the Afghan War, decides to share rooms with the enigmatic Sherlock Holmes, a self-proclaimed consulting detective. Watson desires peace and quiet after his misadventures in Afghanistan but soon discovers that life with Holmes is anything but peaceful. When Miss Mary Morstan calls on Holmes to help solve the mystery of her missing father, the two roommates are soon off on a quest to discover stolen treasure and solve a murder.

Setting:

July 1881 London, various locations

Cast Requirements

For 12 to 21 Cast (7-15 Men, 3-5 women, 2 teen boys)

Characters

Dr. John Watson – former army doctor, 29 years old, home from India due to medical issues stemming from being wounded and contracting enteric fever

Sherlock Holmes – tall, gaunt man, 27 years old, eccentric student of the art of observation and deduction, London's only consulting detective

Stamford – school friend of Watson's, late 20s

- Mary Morstan – young attractive woman, intelligent and even-keeled – she is a governess for another family – her father disappeared 10 years ago, early to late 20s

- Mrs. Hudson – landlady at 221B Baker Street, perpetually exasperated with Holmes

- Wiggins – a boy in his early teens, a street urchin who is the leader of the "Baker Street Irregulars", Holmes' cadre of children detectives

- Thaddeus Sholto – hypochondriac youngest son of the late Major Sholto, dresses exotically in Indian styles

- Bartholomew Sholto – eldest son of the late Major Sholto, paranoid and reclusive, he is dead when we meet him and appears only as a body (no spoken lines)

- Jonathan Small – escaped convict with a lame leg and a wild beard, middle-aged or older, gets about with a crutch

- Tonga – native of the Andaman Islands, short of stature and wild in appearance (no spoken lines)

- Williams – middle-aged prize fighter, works for Thaddeus

- McMurdo – middle-aged prize fighter, works for Bartholomew

- Mrs. Bernstone – elderly woman, Bartholomew's housekeeper

Inspector Abernathy Jones – detective with Scotland Yard, opinionated and not too bright, quickly jumps to conclusions

Mrs. Cecil Forrester – middle-aged woman, she is Mary's employer

Mordecai Smith – middle-aged man, river-boat captain

Mrs. Smith – middle-aged woman, Mordecai's wife

Jack Smith – young son of Mrs. Smith

Constable Murcher – London Police Officer

Captain Pollock – Captain of a Police Launch

Stephenson – Teenaged boy – the "little one" - member of the Baker Street Irregulars

Doubling suggestions:
Wiggins/Tonga

Jack/Stephenson

Stamford/Small

Thaddeus/Mordecai Smith

Williams/Bartholomew/Captain Pollock

McMurdo/Constable Murcher

Mrs. Hudson/Mrs. Forrester

Mrs. Bernstone/Mrs. Smith

SHERLOCK HOLMES AND THE SIGN OF FOUR had its world premiere at the Comtra Theatre in Cranberry Township, PA on May 2, 2014 under the direction of Eric J. McAnallen with the following cast:

Michael Brewer	Sherlock Holmes
Hunter Mehrens	Dr. John Watson
Jenny Mehrens	Mary Morstan
Jim Watson	Stamford/Williams/Bartholomew/Pollock
Kevin McGuire	Inspector Abernathy Jones
Bruce E. Travers	Thaddeus Sholto/Mordecai Smith
Sam Bassett	Wiggins/Tonga
Rachael Rysz	Mrs. Hudson/Mrs. Smith
David Wargo	McMurdo/Murcher
Carl Gross	Jonathan Small
Cathy Gialloreto	Mrs. Bernstone/Mrs. Forrester
Emilia Garcia	Stephenson/Jack Smith

ACT 1

Scene 1 – Dining Room, Holborn Hotel

(Dining room of the Holborn Hotel in London. Two tables are set upstage with patrons and a third table sits downstage center. A waiter goes in and out occasionally, filling drinks and taking orders. Dr. John Watson is seated at the center table by himself reading the London Times. He carries a cane and walks with a limp. Enter Stamford. He sees Watson and recognizes his old friend.)

STAMFORD: Watson, as I do live and breathe.

WATSON: *(Shaking his hand)* Stamford, why I haven't seen you since we were together at Bart's. I was just about to lunch. Why don't you join me?

STAMFORD: I do believe I will. (Sitting) Whatever have you been doing with yourself, Watson? Last I heard, you'd become an army doctor.

WATSON: True enough. Assistant surgeon - attached to the Fifth Northumberland Fusiliers stationed in India.

STAMFORD: Congratulations. I always knew you'd make a good for yourself.

WATSON: Yes, well you may feel differently when I've finished.

STAMFORD: That sounds ominous. Do tell.

WATSON: We were dispatched to Kandahar when the Afghan War broke out.

STAMFORD: That doesn't sound too bad.

WATSON: When I arrived with the other new officers, I was removed from my brigade and attached to the Berkshires.

STAMFORD: *(Realizing the implications)* The Berkshires? Weren't they at the battle of Maiwand? I heard the entire brigade was annihilated.

WATSON: Yes, well during the fighting, I was struck on the shoulder and rendered senseless. My orderly, Murray, threw me over a packhorse and delivered me to British lines or I would have surely perished.

STAMFORD: Well that's a stroke of luck, at least. Was the wound really that terrible?

WATSON: Just as I was improving, I was struck down by enteric fever.

STAMFORD: Enteric fever, nasty stuff. Very common in India from what I hear.

WATSON: It is as nasty as they say. For months, I languished on the verge of death. When I recovered, I was so weak and emaciated that the medical board sent me straight back to England.

STAMFORD: Poor devil!

WATSON: Enough of my misfortune. What about you?

STAMFORD: I've taken a teaching job at the University.

WATSON: Congratulations.

STAMFORD: Thanks, old man. It's good to see you again. What are you up to now?

WATSON: Looking for lodgings. I've been relieved of duty and I'm on half-pay. So, I'm trying to solve the problem as to whether it is possible to get comfortable rooms at a reasonable price.

STAMFORD: That's a strange thing. You are the second man today that has used that expression to me.

WATSON: And who was the first?

STAMFORD: A fellow who is working at the chemical laboratory up at the university. He was bemoaning himself this morning because he could not get someone to go halves with him in some nice rooms.

WATSON: By Jove! If he really wants someone to share the rooms and expense, I am the very man. I should prefer having a partner to being alone.

STAMFORD: You don't know Sherlock Holmes yet. Perhaps you would not care for him as a constant companion.

WATSON: Why, what is there against him?

STAMFORD: Oh, I didn't say there was anything against him. He is a little peculiar in his ideas – an enthusiast in some branches of science. As far as I know he is a decent enough fellow.

WATSON: A medical student, I suppose?

STAMFORD: I believe he is well up in anatomy and he is a first class chemist; but as far as I know, he has never taken any medical classes. His studies are very eccentric.

WATSON: Did you ever ask him what he was going in for?

STAMFORD: No, he is not a man that is easy to draw out, though he can be communicative enough when the fancy seizes him.

WATSON: I should like to meet him. If I am to lodge with anyone, I should prefer a man of studious and quiet habits. I am not strong enough yet to stand much noise or excitement. I had enough of both in Afghanistan to last me for the remainder of my natural existence. How could I meet this friend of yours?

STAMFORD: He is sure to be at the laboratory. I'll stop by after luncheon and see if he would agree to meet us at his lodgings.

WATSON: Certainly.

STAMFORD: You mustn't blame me if you don't get on with him. I know nothing more of him than I have learned from meeting him occasionally at the University. You proposed this arrangement, so you must not hold me responsible.

WATSON: If we don't get on, it will be easy to part company.

STAMFORD: True enough.

WATSON: It seems to me, Stamford, that you have some reason for washing your hands of the matter. Is this fellow's temper so formidable, or what is it? Don't be mealy-mouthed about it.

STAMFORD: It is not easy to express the inexpressible. (Laughs) Holmes is a little too scientific for my tastes. It approaches to cold-bloodedness. I could imagine his giving a friend a little pinch of poison, not out of malevolence, you understand, but simply out of a spirit of inquiry in order to have an accurate idea of the effects. To do him justice, I think that he would take it himself with the same readiness. He appears to have a passion for definite and exact knowledge.

WATSON: Very right too.

STAMFORD: Yes, but it may be pushed to excess. When it comes to beating the cadavers in the dissecting-rooms with a stick, it is certainly taking rather a bizarre shape.

WATSON: Beating the cadavers?

STAMFORD: To verify how far bruises may be produced after death.

WATSON: And yet you say he is not a medical student?

STAMFORD: Heaven knows what the objects of his studies are. You must make your own impressions about him. Now how about that lunch?

END OF SCENE

Scene 2 – 221 B Baker Street

(The sitting rooms at Holmes' lodgings at 221B Baker Street on the second floor of the building. The main entrance to the flat is upstage center. There is a window upstage overlooking the street outside. There is a fireplace upstage right where Holmes keeps his correspondences stuck to the mantelpiece with a jackknife. Also found on the mantle is his pipe and a Persian slipper containing shag tobacco and a cigar box containing cigars. Beside the fireplace is a low bookshelf loaded with books. A tray with whiskey, tonic and glasses sits on the top of the bookshelf. A violin in a case is resting on a chair stage upstage left in the corner. There is a couch and chair center stage around a coffee table. A cart cluttered with chemistry equipment sits downstage right. Holmes is at the cart

experimenting with his back to the door. He is completely drawn into his experiment and does not notice Watson and Stamford enter with Mrs. Hudson.)

MRS HUDSON: The gentlemen you were expecting, Mr. Holmes.

(Holmes waves her off without taking his attention from his experiment.)

MRS HUDSON: He's been at that table all day, Mr. Stamford, sir. I doubt you'll get much more out of him than a few grunts and a wave of his 'and.

STAMFORD: We'll just have to risk it.

MRS HUDSON: If he talks to you, tell him he better eat something. I already took away his breakfast untouched and he hardly glanced at the luncheon tray I left. Mark my words, gentlemen, he'll waste away to nothin' if he don't eat.

STAMFORD: Thank you, Mrs. Hudson. I'm sure we can take it from here.

(Mrs. Hudson exits. Holmes has finally achieved the reaction he wants from his experiment)

HOLMES: *(with a cry of pleasure)* I've found it! I've found it!

(Holmes runs over to Stamford and Watson with exuberance)

HOLMES: I have found a re-agent which is precipitated by hemoglobin, and by nothing else.

STAMFORD: Dr. John Watson, Mr. Sherlock Holmes.

HOLMES: How are you?

(Gripping his hand, Watson grimaces slightly)

You have been in Afghanistan, I perceive.

WATSON: How on earth did you know that?

HOLMES: Never mind *(chuckling to himself)*, the question now is about hemoglobin. No doubt you see the significance of this discovery of mine?

WATSON: It is interesting, chemically, no doubt, but practically…

HOLMES: Why, man, it is the most practical medical-legal discovery for years. Don't you see that it gives us an infallible test for blood stains? Come over here now!

(Holmes seizes Watson by the sleeve and drags him over to the table where he was experimenting.)

Let us have some fresh blood.

(Holmes grabs Watson's finger and pricks it with a lancet he takes from the table and squeezes some blood into a pipette. Watson is too shocked to resist.)

Now I add this small quantity of blood to a liter of water. The resulting mixture has the appearance of pure water and the proportion of blood cannot be more than one in a million. I have no doubt, however, that we shall be able to obtain the characteristic reaction.

(Holmes drops pours some of the water/blood mixture into a flask and then adds the contents of a test tube. In an instant, the contents turn red...See appendix for experiment tips)

Ha! Ha! What do you think of that?

WATSON: *(sucking his finger)* It seems to be a very delicate test.

HOLMES: Beautiful, beautiful! The old test was very clumsy and uncertain and valueless if the stains are a few hours old. Had this test been invented, there are hundreds of men now walking the earth who would long ago have paid the penalty for their crimes.

WATSON: Indeed.

HOLMES: Criminal cases are continually hinging upon that one point. A man is suspected of a crime months after it has been committed. Brownish stains are discovered. Are they blood stains, or mud stains, or rust stains or fruit stains or what are they? That is a question that has puzzled many an expert... and why? Because there was no reliable test. Now we have the Sherlock Holmes test and there will no longer be difficulty.

(Holmes places his hand over his heart and bows as if to some applauding crowd.)

WATSON: You are to be congratulated.

STAMFORD: We came here on business.

(Stamford sits down and motions for Holmes and Watson to join him.)

My friend here wants to take diggings and as you were complaining that you could get no one to go halves with you, I thought that I had better bring you together.

HOLMES: There's plenty of room here on Baker Street and this should suit two down to the ground. My bedroom is through there and yours would be there. You don't mind the smell of strong tobacco, I hope?

WATSON: I always smoke ship's myself.

HOLMES: That's good enough. I generally have chemicals about and occasionally do experiments. *(Waving at his equipment)* Would that annoy you?

WATSON: By no means.

HOLMES: Let me see… what are my other shortcomings? I get in the dumps at times and don't open my mouth for days on end. You must not think I am sulky when I do that. Just let me alone and I'll soon be alright. What have you to confess now? It's just as well for two fellows to know the worst of one another before they begin to live together.

WATSON: *(Laughing)* I keep a bull pup and I object to rows because my nerves are shaken and I get up at all sorts of ungodly hours and I am extremely lazy. I have another set of vices when I am well, but those are the principal ones at present.

HOLMES: Do you include playing the violin in your category of rows?

WATSON: Depends on the player. A well-played violin is a treat for the gods. A badly played one…

HOLMES: *(Laughing)* Oh that's all right. I think we may consider the thing as settled, that is if the rooms are agreeable to you.

WATSON: They are.

HOLMES: Excellent. I shall fetch the landlady for the arrangements.

(Holmes leaves.)

WATSON: How the deuce did he know that I had come from Afghanistan?

STAMFORD: That's just his little peculiarity. A good many people have wanted to know how he finds things out.

WATSON: Oh, a mystery is it? This is very piquant. I am much obliged to you for bringing us together. The proper study of mankind is man, you know.

STAMFORD: You must study him then. You'll find him a mystifying problem, though. I'll wager he learns more about you than you about him.

END OF SCENE

Scene 3 – 221 B Baker Street

(221B Baker Street. It is six weeks later. The cart with the chemistry equipment has been removed. Holmes and Wiggins are standing by the door and in mid-discussion as the lights come up.)

HOLMES: *(Handing him a package)* These papers are for Lestrade. Take them down to him at once. Tell him Sherlock Holmes sent you. Bring his attention to the Brixton Road case. He should be able to put the rest of it together from that.

WIGGINS: Yes, guv'nor.

HOLMES: Good, boy. Be sure to come right back here and tell me what he says.

WIGGINS: Certainly, Mr. 'olmes. Will you be needin' the rest of the boys?

HOLMES: No, Wiggins, not today, I think. But we will discuss that when you return.

(As Wiggins and Holmes are speaking, Watson enters from his bedroom and catches the last part of the discussion. Wiggins leaves and Holmes fetches his violin and starts playing - something by Mendelssohn, Chopin or Paganini. Watson sits and starts reading a magazine.)

HOLMES: *(Stopping abruptly)* Sorry about putting you to an inconvenience these past six weeks. I have clients to attend to. I have to use this room as a place of business. It's good of you to understand.

WATSON: Not at all.

(Holmes goes back to playing and Watson continues reading the magazine.)

(After a bit) Listen to this. *(Reading from magazine)*

"By a man's finger nails, by his coat sleeves, by his boots, by his trouser knees, by the callosities of his forefinger and thumb, by his expression, by his shirt cuffs… by each of these things a man's calling is plainly revealed. That all united should fail to enlighten the competent inquirer in any case is almost inconceivable."

What ineffable twaddle. I have never read such rubbish in my life.

HOLMES: You don't say?

WATSON: I don't deny that it is smartly written but it is not practical. Evidently the theory of some armchair lounger who evolves neat little paradoxes in the seclusion of his own study. I would like to see him clapped down in a third class carriage in the Underground and asked to give the trades of all his fellow travelers. I would lay a thousand to one against him.

HOLMES: You would lose your money. As for the article, I wrote it myself.

WATSON: You?!

HOLMES: Yes, I have a turn both for observation and for deduction. The theories which I have expressed there and which appear to you to be so chimerical are really extremely practical. So practical that I depend upon them for my bread and cheese.

WATSON: And how?

HOLMES: Well, I have a trade of my own. I suppose I am the only one in the world. I'm a consulting detective. Here in London we have lots of government detectives and lots of private ones. When these fellows are baffled, they come to me and I manage to put them on the right scent. They lay all the evidence before me and I am generally able to set them straight.

WATSON: But do you mean to say that without leaving this room you can unravel some knot which other men can make nothing of?

HOLMES: Quite so. I have a kind of intuition that way.

WATSON: So these people you have been seeing…?

HOLMES: Clients, agents, detectives. Take my latest client, Lestrade. He is a well-known detective for Scotland Yard. He got himself into a fog recently over a forgery case and that was what brought him to me.

WATSON: And the other people?

HOLMES: They are mostly sent by private agencies. I listen to their story, they listen to my comments and then I pocket my fee. Those rules of deduction laid down in that article which aroused your scorn are invaluable to me in practical work.

WATSON: I don't see how.

HOLMES: Let me give an example. You appeared to be surprised when I told you on our first meeting that you had come from Afghanistan.

WATSON: You were told, no doubt.

HOLMES: Nothing of the sort. I knew you came from Afghanistan. The train of reasoning ran, here is a gentleman of a medical type, but with the air of a military man. Clearly an army doctor. He has just come from the tropics for his face is dark and that is not the natural tint of his skin for his wrists are fair. He has undergone some hardship and sickness as his haggard face says clearly. His left arm has been injured for he holds it in a stiff and unnatural manner and he walks with a limp. Where in the tropics could an English army doctor have seen much hardship and got wounded? Clearly, Afghanistan.

WATSON: It's simple enough as you explain it. You have an extraordinary genius for minutiae.

HOLMES: I appreciate their importance.

(Wiggins enters)

WIGGINS: Pardon, sir, Mr. 'olmes. But you said you wanted to know what Inspector Lestrade had to say.

HOLMES: Excuse us, Doctor. *(To Wiggins)* Out with it.

WIGGINS: He said the matter is in good 'ands and he'll have the residence searched again.

HOLMES: No, that won't do. It will only arouse more suspicion.

(Holmes writes out an address one paper and some directions on another.)

Looks like we'll need some of the boys after all. Here, send two of them to this address. I think Murphy and the little one.

WIGGINS: Stephenson?

HOLMES: Yes, that's the one. Have one watch the back door and the other the front. They are to take this note to Lestrade if a slight, middle-aged woman with red hair comes or goes. Understood?

WIGGINS: Yes sir.

HOLMES: We'll help Lestrade solve his case, despite of himself, eh Wiggins?

WIGGINS: You bet, Mr. 'olmes sir. We'll get him straight.

HOLMES: *(handing him some coins)* Here are your wages, now off you go.

(Wiggins exits)

WATSON: What on earth was that about?

HOLMES: Wiggins is the representative of the Baker Street irregular division of the detective police force.

WATSON: Am I to understand that you employ children?

HOLMES: There's more work to be got out of one of those little beggars than out of a dozen of the force. The mere sight of an official-looking person seals men's lips. These youngsters go everywhere and hear everything. They are as sharp as needles too; all they want is organization. Now where were we?

WATSON: Discussing your most unusual profession.

HOLMES: I'm sure I weary you with my hobby.

WATSON: Not at all. It is of the greatest interest to me. Would you think me impertinent if I were to put your theories to a more severe test?

HOLMES: I should be delighted.

WATSON: What did the article say? *(Picking up magazine and reading)* Here it is.

"It is difficult for a man to have any object in daily use without leaving the impress of his individuality upon it in such a way that a trained observer might read it."

Now, here I have a watch which has recently come into my possession. Would you kindly let me have an opinion upon the character of the late owner?

(Watson hands Holmes a pocket watch. Holmes examines the watch in great detail, even taking a magnifying glass out to look at it closer and opening the back of the case to look inside.)

HOLMES: There are hardly any data. The watch has been recently cleaned which robs me of my most suggestive facts.

(Hands the watch back to Watson)

WATSON: You are right. It was cleaned before being sent to me.

HOLMES: Though unsatisfactory, my research has not been entirely barren. I should judge that the watch belonged to your elder brother who inherited it from your father.

WATSON: That you gather, no doubt from the H. W. upon the back.

HOLMES: Quite so. The W suggests your own name. The date on the watch is nearly fifty years back and the initials are as old as the watch so it was made for the last generation. Jewelry usually descends to the eldest son. Your father has, if I remember right, been dead many years. It has therefore been in the hands of your eldest brother.

WATSON: Right so far. Anything else?

HOLMES: He was a man of untidy habits, very untidy and careless. He was left with good prospects but he threw away his chances, lived for some time in poverty with occasional short intervals of prosperity and finally taking to drink, he died. That is all I can gather.

WATSON: *(Jumping up, visibly upset)* This is unworthy of you, Holmes. I could not believe you would have descended to making inquiries into the history of my unhappy brother and now you pretend to deduce this knowledge in some fanciful way. You cannot expect me to believe that you read all that from his old watch.

HOLMES: My dear doctor, pray accept my apologies. Viewing the matter as an abstract problem, I had forgotten how personal and painful a thing it might have been to you. I assure you, however, that I never even knew you had a brother until you handed me that watch.

WATSON: Then how in the name of all that is wonderful did you get these facts? They are absolutely correct in every particular.

HOLMES: Ah, that is good luck. I did not expect to be so accurate.

WATSON: But it was not mere guesswork?

HOLMES: No, no. I never guess... destructive to the logical faculty. I started by saying your brother was careless. If you observe the lower part of the watch case, you notice that it is not only dinted in two places but it is cut and marked all over from the habit of keeping other hard objects, such as coins or keys in the same pocket. Surely it is no great feat to assume that a man who treats a fifty guinea watch so cavalierly must be careless. Neither is it a very far-fetched inference that a man who inherits such a watch was pretty well provided for.

WATSON: That is true.

HOLMES: It is customary for pawnbrokers to scratch the ticket number upon the inside of the case. There are no less than four such numbers visible to my lens on the inside of that watch. Inference... your brother was often at low water. Secondary inference... he occasionally had bursts of prosperity or he could not have redeemed the watch. Finally, I ask you to look at the thousands of scratches around the keyhole... marks where the key has slipped. You will never see a drunkard's watch without them.

WATSON: It is clear as daylight. I regret the injustice I did you.

(There is a knock and Mrs. Hudson enters)

HOLMES: Elementary, Doctor.

MRS HUDSON: Pardon me, gentlemen.

WATSON: Ah, Mrs. Hudson, do come in.

MRS HUDSON: I hope I'm not interrupting, Doctor. It sounded like quite the discussion downstairs.

WATSON: Don't worry yourself, Mrs. Hudson. We were just discussing my brother's watch.

HOLMES: What do you need?

WATSON: Nothing like getting to the point, eh Holmes?

MRS HUDSON: There's a young lady for you, sir.

(She hands Holmes a card.)

HOLMES: Miss Mary Morstan. Hum! I have no recollection of that name. Did she say what she wanted?

MRS HUDSON: I never think to ask, sir. You know that.

HOLMES: Indeed, Mrs. Hudson, I do. Ask the young lady to step up.

MRS HUDSON: Yes, sir.

(Watson starts to leave)

HOLMES: Don't go, Doctor. I should prefer that you remain.

(Mary enters. She is calm and collected but has the air of one who is intensely agitated inwardly. She takes the seat Holmes offers.)

Miss Morstan, I am Sherlock Holmes and this is my associate, Dr. Watson, recently returned from service in Afghanistan.

MISS MORSTAN: How do you do, Doctor?

WATSON: A pleasure.

HOLMES: Please, have a seat.

> *(Watson shakes her hand awkwardly. Holmes takes his violin to put it back in its case. Watson takes the opportunity to seat himself on the couch beside Mary.)*

MISS MORSTAN: I have come to you, Mr. Holmes because you once enabled my employer, Mrs. Cecil Forrester, to unravel a little domestic complication. She was much impressed by your kindness and skill.

> *(While she speaks, Watson is watching her intently. He is obviously smitten.)*

HOLMES: Mrs. Cecil Forrester. I believe that I was of some slight service to her. The case, however, was a very simple one.

MISS MORSTAN: She did not think so. But at least you cannot say the same of mine. I can hardly imagine anything more strange, more utterly inexplicable, than the situation in which I find myself.

HOLMES: State your case.

WATSON: *(Rising)* You will, I am sure, excuse me.

MISS MORSTAN: *(Holding up her hand to detain Watson)* If the Doctor would be good enough to stay, he might be of inestimable service to me.

(Watson sits back down.)

MISS MORSTAN: Briefly, the facts are these. My father was an officer in an Indian Regiment. My mother died in childbirth and I had no relative in England. I was placed, however, in a comfortable boarding establishment at Edinburgh and there I remained until I was seventeen. In 1871 Papa obtained leave and came home. He telegraphed me that he had arrived in London and directed me to come down at once, giving his address as the Langham Hotel. I arrived at the Langham and was told Captain Morstan had gone out the night before and had not returned. I waited all day without news. I communicated with the police and the next morning we advertised in all the papers. Our inquiry led to no results and from that day to this, no word has been heard from my unfortunate father. He came home with his heart full of hope to find some peace, some comfort and instead...

(She puts her hand to her throat and a choking sob cuts short the sentence. Watson leans forward to put a hand on her shoulder to comfort her. He pulls a handkerchief from his sleeve[1] and offers it to Mary. She uses it to wipe away some tears.)

---

[1] Watson still has the military habit of keeping the handkerchief in the sleeve. In Sherlock Holmes canon, Holmes often berates Watson for doing this.

MISS MORSTAN: Thank you, Doctor. You are too kind.

HOLMES: The date?

MISS MORSTAN: He disappeared upon the third of December, 1871, nearly ten years ago.

HOLMES: His luggage?

MISS MORSTAN: Remained at the hotel. There was nothing in it to suggest a clue, just some clothes, some books and a considerable number of curiosities from the Andaman Islands. He had been one of the officers in charge of the convict-guard at Port Blair.

HOLMES: Had he any friends in town?

MISS MORSTAN: Only one that we know of – Major Sholto, of the same regiment. The Major had retired some little time before and lived at Upper Norwood. We communicated with him, of course, but he did not even know that my father was in England.

HOLMES: A bizarre case.

MISS MORSTAN: I have not yet described to you the most bizarre part. About six years ago – to be exact, upon the fourth of May, 1875 – there arrived a small cardboard box which I found to contain a very large and lustrous pearl.

WATSON: How peculiar. Was there a note?

MISS MORSTAN: Nothing. No word of writing was enclosed. Since then every year upon the same date there has appeared a similar box containing a similar pearl. You can see for yourself that they are very handsome.

(She opens a box of pearls and passes it to Holmes. He examines them briefly and passes them to Watson.)

WATSON: Those are six of the finest pearls I have ever seen.

HOLMES: Your statement is most interesting. Has anything else occurred?

MISS MORSTAN: Yes, and no later than today. That is why I have come to you. This morning I received this letter.

(Mary hands the letter to Holmes.)

HOLMES: Thank you. The envelope too, please. *(Examining)* Postmark, London, Date July 7. Hum! Man's thumb mark on corner – probably postman, Best quality paper. Envelopes at sixpence a packet. Particular man in his stationary. Smells faintly of sage and Indian tobacco. No address.

(Holmes reads the letter.)

"Be at the third pillar from the left outside the Lyceum Theatre tonight at seven o'clock. If you are distrustful, bring two friends. You are a wronged woman and shall have justice. Do not bring police. If you do, all will be in vain. Your unknown friend."

Well, this is a very pretty little mystery. What do you intend to do, Miss Morstan?

MISS MORSTAN: That is exactly what I want to ask you.

HOLMES: Then we shall most certainly go – you and I and – yes, why Dr. Watson is the very man. Your correspondent says two friends.

MISS MORSTAN: But would he come?

WATSON: I shall be proud and happy if I can be of any service.

MISS MORSTAN: You are both very kind. If I meet you at the Lyceum at 6:30, it will do, I suppose?

HOLMES: There is one other point, however. Is this handwriting the same as that upon the pearl-box addresses?

MISS MORSTAN: I have them here.

HOLMES: You are certainly a model client. You have the correct intuition. Let us see now. *(Spreading the papers out on the table)* They are disguised hands, except the letter, but there can be no question as to authorship. See how the irrepressible Greek 'e' will break out and see the twirl on the final 's'. They are undoubtedly by the same person. I should not like to suggest false hopes but is there any resemblance between this hand and that of your father?

MISS MORSTAN: Nothing could be more unalike.

HOLMES: I expected as much. We shall look for you at 6:30. Pray allow me to keep the papers, I may look into the matter before then. Au revoir.

MISS MORSTAN: Au revoir.

(Watson shows Mary to the door and watches out the window as she departs.)

WATSON: What a very attractive woman.

HOLMES: *(Lighting his pipe)* Is she? I did not observe.

WATSON: You really are an automaton – a calculating machine. There is something positively inhuman in you at times.

HOLMES: *(Smiling)* It is of the first importance to not allow your judgment to be biased by personal qualities. I assure you that the most winning woman I ever knew was hanged for poisoning three children and the most repellent man of my acquaintance is a philanthropist who has spent nearly a quarter of a million upon the London poor.

WATSON: In this case, however…

HOLMES: I never make exceptions. An exception disproves the rule. *(Holmes gestures to the letter)* Have you ever had an occasion to study handwriting? What do you make of this fellow's scribble?

WATSON: It is legible and regular. A man of business habits and some force of character.

HOLMES: *(Shaking his head)* Look at his long letters. They hardly rise above the common herd. That 'd' might be an 'a' and that 'i' an 'e'. Men of character always differentiate their long letters. No, this is a peculiar man, not accustomed to getting his way. A bit demure, used to be overshadowed by someone greater, a father or an older brother, perhaps.

WATSON: And you got that from the handwriting?

HOLMES: Indeed. I am going out now. I have some references to make. I shall meet you at the Lyceum.

(Holmes collects the papers, grabs his coat and hat and heads for the door leaving Watson.)

END OF SCENE

Scene 4 – Outside Lyceum Theatre

(Outside the Lyceum Theatre. Watson is alone, waiting. Patrons are hustling and bustling about on their way to the theatre. A paperboy enters, selling papers. Williams enters. He is a rough looking man, dressed as a coachman. He is searching the crowd looking for Mary. Not finding her, he leaves. As he leaves,

Holmes enters and passes Williams on the way out. Watson sees Holmes and calls him over. People continue to pass while Holmes and Watson speak.)

WATSON: Over here, Holmes. Well, did your inquiries bear fruit?

HOLMES: There is no great mystery in this matter. The facts appear to admit of only one explanation.

WATSON: What? Have you solved it already?

HOLMES: Well, that would be too much to say. I have discovered a suggestive fact is all. I found on consulting the Times that Major Sholto died upon the twenty-eight of April, 1875.

WATSON: I may be very obtuse, Holmes, but I fail to see what this suggests.

HOLMES: No? You surprise me. Look at it this way, then. Captain Morstan disappears. The only person in London whom he could have visited is Major Sholto. The Major denies having heard he was in London. Four years later, Sholto dies. Within a week of his death, Captain Morstan's daughter received a valuable present which is repeated each year culminating in a letter which describes her as a wronged woman. What wrong can it refer to except this deprivation of her father? And why should the presents begin immediately after Sholto's death unless it is that Sholto's heir knows something of the mystery and wishes to make compensation?

WATSON: But what strange compensation! And how strangely made. Why too should he write a letter now rather than six years ago? Again the letter speaks of giving her justice. What justice can she have? It is too much to suppose that her father is still alive. There is no other injustice in her case that you know of.

HOLMES: There are difficulties; there are certainly difficulties. Sholto had two heirs, the eldest son, Bartholomew still lives in the family estate in Upper Norwood while the younger son, Thaddeus, has dropped from view.

WATSON: Do you think the letter and pearls came from this Thaddeus?

HOLMES: You're catching on, Doctor. I do indeed think that. Ah, here is Miss Morstan.

(Mary has entered and joins Holmes and Watson. Williams has followed her on and waits off to one side, attempting to blend while he eavesdrops.)

MISS MORSTAN: Good evening, Gentlemen.

WATSON: Good evening.

HOLMES: Miss Morstan, what relationship did your father have with Major Sholto, if you don't mind me asking?

MISS MORSTAN: Major Sholto was a very good friend of Papa's. He and Papa were in command of the troops at Port Blair so they were together a great deal.

By the way, a curious paper was found in Papa's desk which no one could understand. I don't suppose it is of the slightest importance but I thought you might care to see it, so I brought it with me.

(Mary hands Holmes the paper. He unfolds it carefully and then examines it with his lens.)

HOLMES: It is paper of native Indian manufacture. It has some time been pinned to a board. The diagram appears to be a plan of a large building with numerous halls and passages. At one point is a small cross done in red ink and above it is 3.37 from the left in faded pencil writing. In the left-hand corner is a curious hieroglyphic like four crosses in a line with their arms touching. Beside it is written, "The sign of four – Jonathan Small, Mohamet Singh, Abdullah Kahn, Dost Akbar." No, I confess, I do not see how this bears upon the matter. Yet it is evidently an important document. It has been carefully kept in a pocketbook, for one side is clean as the other.

MISS MORSTAN: It was in Papa's pocketbook when we found it.

HOLMES: Preserve it carefully, Miss Morstan, for it may be of use to us. I begin to suspect this matter may turn out to be much deeper and more subtle than I supposed. I must reconsider my ideas.

WATSON: Holmes, there's a coachman just over there who's been eying us up for the past several minutes.

HOLMES: Yes, I noticed him earlier. Be on guard, Watson.

(Williams approaches the group. He looks over Holmes and Watson as if weighing them up. Mary moves behind Watson and Holmes and they stand between her and Williams as protectors.)

WILLIAMS: Are you the parties who come with Miss Morstan?

MISS MORSTAN: I am Miss Morstan, and these two gentlemen are my friends.

WILLIAMS: You will excuse me, miss, but I was to ask you to give me your word that neither of your companions is a police-officer.

MISS MORSTAN: I give you my word on that.

WILLIAMS: *(Whistling for the cab)* Very well, then come with me.

WATSON: Never fear, Miss Morstan, we are with you.

(All exit)

END OF SCENE

Scene 5 – Home of Thaddeus Sholto

(Home of Thaddeus Sholto. It is decorated with Oriental and Indian art. A short table is in the middle of the room with a Hookah upon it.

There are cushions around the table for sitting. The whole place gives the impression of Eastern luxury. Thaddeus is seated at the head of the table and is oddly dressed in the manner of an Oriental prince. There is a knock on the door. Williams enters, leading Holmes, Watson and Mary)

WILLIAMS: Miss Morstan and friends.

SHOLTO: Show them in to me, Williams. Show them straight in to me.

(Thaddeus rises to meet them and extends his hand. Holmes and Watson shield Mary from Thaddeus, still unsure of his motives.)

Your servant, Miss Morstan. Your servant, gentleman. Pray step into my little sanctum. A small place but furnished to my own liking. A small oasis of art in the howling desert of South London. Mr. Thaddeus Sholto. That is my name. You are Miss Morstan, of course. And these gentlemen?

MISS MORSTAN: This is Mr. Sherlock Holmes and Dr. Watson.

SHOLTO: A doctor, eh? Have you your stethoscope? Might I ask you – would you have the kindness? I have grave doubts as to my mitral valve, if you would be so good. The aortic I may rely upon but I should value your opinion on the mitral.

(Watson takes out his stethoscope and listens to Thaddeus' heart.)

WATSON: It appears to be normal. You have no cause for uneasiness.

SHOLTO: You will excuse my anxiety, Miss Morstan. I am a great sufferer and I have long had suspicions to that valve. I am delighted to hear they are unwarranted. Had your father, Miss Morstan, refrained from throwing strain upon his heart, he might have been alive now.

(Mary is visibly shaken and Watson is offended by the callousness of Thaddeus' remark.)

WATSON: Here, now!

SHOLTO: Oh… sorry. I had not meant to offend the young lady.

MISS MORSTAN: It's all right, Mr. Sholto. I knew in my heart that he was dead.

SHOLTO: Please, sit.

(Watson helps Mary to one of the cushions and sits beside her. Thaddeus returns to his seat and Holmes sits in the remaining seat.)

SHOLTO: I can give you every information and what is more, I can do you justice, whatever Brother Bartholomew may say. But let us have no outsiders – no police or officials. Nothing would annoy Brother Bartholomew more than publicity.

HOLMES: For my part, whatever you may choose to say will go no further.

(Watson nods in agreement)

SHOLTO: That is well! That is well! May I offer you a glass of Chianti, Miss Morstan? Or of Tokay? Shall I open a flask? No? Well then, I trust that you have no objection to tobacco-smoke, to the balsamic odor of the Eastern tobacco? When I am nervous, I find my hookah an invaluable sedative.

(Thaddeus picks up his hookah pipe and begins puffing away at it.)

When I first determined to make this communication, I might have given you my address but I was afraid you'd bring unpleasant people with you. That is why I sent Williams to meet you first. He had orders that if he were dissatisfied to proceed no further. I seldom come in contact with the rough crowd. I live, as you see, with some little atmosphere of elegance. I may call myself a patron of the arts.

MISS MORSTAN: You will excuse me, Mr. Sholto, but I am here at your request to learn something which you wish to tell me. It is very late and I should desire the interview to be short as possible.

SHOLTO: At the best, it must take some time for we shall certainly have to go to Norwood, to Pondicherry Lodge, to see Brother Bartholomew. He is very angry with me for taking the course which seemed right to me.

WATSON: If we are to go to Norwood, it would be as well to start at once.

SHOLTO: *(Laughing)* That would hardly do. No, I must prepare you. My father, as you all know, was Major John Sholto. He retired some eleven years ago and brought home with him a considerable sum of money, a large collection of valuable curiosities and a staff of native servants.

HOLMES: This we know.

SHOLTO: Yes. Well, I remember the sensation that was caused when your father, Captain Morstan disappeared. Knowing father had been his friend, we freely discussed it in his presence. He used to join in our speculations. Never did we suspect that he had the whole secret hidden in his own breast. Yet, we knew that there was some mystery that hung over father. He was always fearful of going out alone and employed two prize-fighters to act as porters. Williams was one of them. He was once lightweight champion of England.

HOLMES: Any idea what made you father fearful to venture out?

SHOLTO: Father never told us what he feared, but he had an aversion to lame men with crutches, once firing upon a lame man who proved to be a harmless tradesman. We had to pay a large sum to hush that up. Are you sure I can't interest anyone in a drink?

MISS MORSTAN: Mr. Sholto, please.

SHOLTO: Yes... um, where was I?

WATSON: Lame man, cover up, your father...

SHOLTO: Oh, right... In 1875, father received a letter from India which was a great shock to him. He sickened to his death. He called us to his deathbed and grasping our hands, he made a remarkable statement. I shall try to give it to you in his own words.

"I have only one thing that weighs upon my mind. It is my treatment of poor Morstan's orphan. The cursed greed which has been my sin has kept from her half the treasure which should have been hers. You, my sons, will give her a share of the Agra treasure."

WATSON: So he had intended to make amends.

SHOLTO: Yes, but he made us swear we wouldn't do anything until after he had died. He had taken out a chaplet with the intention of sending it to Miss Morstan.

HOLMES: And the chaplet is the source of the pearls?

SHOLTO: True enough. You see, father and Captain Morstan had come into possession of a considerable treasure which was brought back to England by father. When Morstan came for his share, he and father argued over the division of the treasure.

WATSON: So your father killed him?

HOLMES: Please, Watson, no speculation until we have all the facts.

SHOLTO: No, you see that is exactly what he thought everyone would say. In his anger, Morstan stressed his weak heart and died. Father knew he would be accused of murder so he concealed the body as well as the treasure. He was about to tell us where the treasure was hidden when he saw someone at the window. "Keep him out! For God's sake, keep him out!" he cried. We turned to the window where his gaze was fixed and there was a face staring back at us. We rushed the window but he was gone. When we returned to father, his head had dropped and his pulse had ceased to beat.

HOLMES: Can you describe this face in the window?

SHOLTO: It was a bearded, hairy face with wild cruel eyes and an expression of concentrated malevolence. That's the best I can do. I only saw it briefly.

HOLMES: Anything else unusual about that night.

SHOLTO: Not so much that night, but in the morning, we discovered father's bedroom window had been forced open and the cupboards and chests had been rifled. Upon father's chest was fixed a torn piece of paper with the words "The Sign of Four" scrawled across it.

WATSON: Are you well, Miss Morstan? You have turned deadly white. I fear you may faint.

MISS MORSTAN: No, I shall be fine, Doctor.

HOLMES: The Sign of Four. You're sure that's what was written?

SHOLTO: Of course, I will never forget it nor that horrid face.

HOLMES: What of the treasure?

SHOLTO: For weeks and for months we dug and delved every part of the grounds without discovering its hiding place. It was maddening to think he was just about to tell us when he died. We could judge the splendor of the treasure from the chaplet. Brother Bartholomew and I had some disagreement over the disposition of this chaplet. You see, he is a little inclined to my father's fault. It was all I could do to persuade him to send Miss Morstan a pearl at fixed intervals so that she might never feel destitute.

MISS MORSTAN: That was a kindly thought. It was extremely good of you.

SHOLTO: We were your trustees. Or that was the view I took of it, though Brother Bartholomew could not altogether see the light.

WATSON: So what has changed that you contact Miss Morstan now?

HOLMES: The treasure has been found.

SHOLTO: Precisely.

WATSON: And how was it found after all this time.

SHOLTO: Brother Bartholomew is a clever fellow. He came to the conclusion that it was hidden indoors so he worked out all the cubic space of the house. He found that the height of the building was seventy-four feet but the height of the rooms all added together, even accounting for space between, did not total more than seventy feet. There were four feet unaccounted for. He knocked a hole in the highest room and there sure enough he came upon another little garret that was sealed up and known to no one. He found the chest resting on two rafters. He calculates the jewels at not less than half a million sterling.

HOLMES: Even a third of that would make Miss Morstan the wealthiest heiress in England.

SHOLTO: Indeed.

HOLMES: You have done well sir, from first to last. We had best put the matter through without delay.

(Williams brings Thaddeus a long topcoat which he buttons completely up.)

SHOLTO: Williams, ready the coach. We are headed for Pondicherry Lodge.

WILLIAMS: At once, sir.

WATSON: It's a warm night. I don't think you will need quite a...

SHOLTO: My health is quite fragile, Doctor. Quite fragile. Shall we go?

END OF SCENE

Scene 6 – Entrance Gate, Pondicherry Lodge

(Entrance gate to the grounds at Pondicherry Lodge. McMurdo enters when there is a knocking at the gate.)

MCMURDO: Who is there?

SHOLTO: *(From outside)* It is I, McMurdo. You surely know my knock by this time.

(McMurdo lets in Thaddeus, Holmes, Watson and Mary.)

MCMURDO: That you, Mr. Thaddeus? But who are these others? I had no orders about them from the master.

SHOLTO: No, McMurdo? You surprise me! I told my brother last night I should bring some friends.

MCMURDO: He hain't been out o' his rooms to-day, Mr. Thaddeus, and I have no orders. You know very well that I must stick to regulations. I can let you in but your friends must stop where they are.

SHOLTO: If I guarantee them, is that enough for you?

MCMURDO: Very sorry, Mr. Thaddeus. Folk may be friends o' yours and yet no friend o' the master's. He pays me well to do my duty and my duty I'll do. I don't know none o' your friends.

HOLMES: Oh yes you do, McMurdo. I don't think you can have forgotten me. Don't you remember that amateur who fought three rounds with you at Alison's rooms on the night of your benefit four years back?

MCMURDO: Not Mr. Sherlock Holmes! God's truth! How could I have mistook you? If instead o' standin' there so quiet you had just stepped up and given me that cross-hit of yours under the jaw, I'd ha' known you without question. Ah, you're the one that has wasted your gifts, you have! You might have aimed high, if you had joined the fancy!

HOLMES: You see, Watson, if all else fails me, I have still one of the scientific professions open to me.

WATSON: You do astound me, Holmes.

HOLMES: Our friend won't keep us out in the cold now, I'm sure.

MCMURDO: In you come, sir, in you come – you and your friends. Very sorry, Mr. Thaddeus, but orders are very strict. Had to be certain of your friends before I let them in.

SHOLTO: McMurdo, Williams is in the street with the carriage. Can you kindly open the service gate so he can pull it around back?

MCMURDO: Right away, sir.

SHOLTO: I cannot understand it. There must be some mistake. I distinctly told Bartholomew that we should be here and yet there is no light in his window. I do not know what to make of it.

HOLMES: Does he always guard the premises in this way?

SHOLTO: Yes, he followed in my father's custom. He was father's favorite and sometimes I think he may have told him more than he told me. That is Bartholomew's window up there where the moonshine strikes. There is no light within, I think.

HOLMES: None. But I see a glint of light in that little window by the door.

SHOLTO: Ah, that's the housekeeper's room where old Mrs. Bernstone sits. She can tell us about it. Wait here, I shall be back in a moment.

(Mary has taken Watson's hand and stands close to him for comfort.)

MISS MORSTAN: What a strange place. It looks as though all the moles in England had been let loose in it. I have seen something of the sort on the side of a hill near Ballrat where prospectors had been at work.

HOLMES: And from the same cause. These are the traces of the treasure seekers. You must remember that they were six years looking for it. No wonder the grounds look like a gravel pit.

(Thaddeus enters a bit frenzied)

SHOLTO: There is something amiss with Bartholomew! I am frightened! My nerves cannot stand it.

HOLMES: *(Firmly)* Come into the house.

SHOLTO: Yes, do! I really do not feel equal to giving directions.

(Holmes, Watson, Mary and Thaddeus head off towards the house.)

END OF SCENE

Scene 7 – Bartholomew's Room, Pondicherry Lodge

(Bartholomew's room. The stage is split so that there is a door mid-stage to give the impression of seeing inside the room and in the hallway at the same time. There is a closed window and a door leading to a dressing room. Bartholomew is slumped back in his chair, dead, facing the door. Holmes, Watson, Mary and Thaddeus are shown in by Mrs. Bernstone.)

MRS BERNSTONE: Oh, Mr. Thaddeus, sir. I am so glad you have come! I am so glad you have come, Mr. Thaddeus, sir! Mr. Bartholomew hasn't been out of his room all day.

SHOLTO: *(Knocking on the door and trying the handle)* Brother Bartholomew? It's locked.

MRS BERNSTONE: Master has locked himself in and will not answer me. All day I have waited to hear from him for he often likes to be alone but now I think something is amiss.

HOLMES: Is there a key to this door?

MRS BERNSTONE: Only the one, sir, and Mr. Bartholomew always keeps it on him.

WATSON: Are we sure Mr. Sholto is in there?

MRS BERNSTONE: *(Kneeling down to look in the keyhole)* Mr. Bartholomew, sir. Are you in there? Your brother and some friends are here.

(Upon seeing Bartholomew's face through the keyhole, Mrs. Bernstone gives out a scream and falls back away from the door.)

WATSON: My, dear lady, what's the matter.

MRS BERNSTONE: It's horrible. Never have I seen a face like that.

HOLMES: Miss Morstan, take Mrs. Bernstone downstairs.

MISS MORSTAN: Come with me, Mrs. Bernstone. We'll get you some water.

(Mary and Mrs. Bernstone exit)

HOLMES: There is something devilish in this, Watson. What do you make of it?

WATSON: *(Looking through the keyhole)* There is a man seated at a desk. Judging from the expression on the face, I'd say he's dead. This must be what frightened Mrs. Bernstone. This is terrible! What is to be done?

(Holmes pulls a case containing lock picking tools out of his breast pocket and proceeds to pick the lock. When he finally gets it to open, he takes the lantern from Watson and enters.)

HOLMES: Wait here by the door.

(Holmes goes to the body and checks for a pulse. He searches the body carefully and finds a note pinned to his back. He waves for Watson.)

You see?

WATSON: *(Reading)* The sign of four. In God's name, what does it all mean?

HOLMES: It means murder. *(Stooping over the dead man)* Ah, I expected it. Look here!

WATSON: It looks like a thorn.

HOLMES: It is a thorn. You may pick it out but be careful for it is poisoned.

(Watson pulls the thorn out of the body, takes a handkerchief from his pocket and carefully wraps up the thorn.)

WATSON: This is all an insoluble mystery to me. It grows darker instead of lighter.

HOLMES: On the contrary, it clears every instant. I only require a few missing links to have an entirely connected case.

(Holmes goes the lantern hanging in the corner to light it. His back is to Watson. In the meantime, Watson pushes the body down onto the desk and drapes a nearby blanket over him.)

What are you doing, Doctor?

WATSON: Showing some respect to the dead.

HOLMES: In the future, Watson, you will refrain from disturbing the crime scene before I've had a chance to fully examine it. Well, since you have handled the body, what is your estimate of the time of death?

WATSON: Hard to say without more instruments but if I had to estimate…

HOLMES: You do.

WATSON: I'd say Mr. Sholto has been dead for at least a day.

HOLMES: That was my estimate as well.

(All this time, Thaddeus has been standing in the doorway with a look of terror, wringing his hands and moaning to himself.)

SHOLTO: The treasure is gone. They have robbed him of the treasure. The hole through which we lowered it is in the dressing room, through there. I helped him to carry it - here. I was the last person who saw him! I left him here last night and I heard him lock the door as I came down the stairs.

HOLMES: What time was that?

SHOLTO: It was ten o'clock.

HOLMES: So that puts the murder at some time last night after you departed. Does the dressing room connect to any other rooms?

SHOLTO: No, it's just a small room with a chair and no windows. Oh, dear! Oh, dear! Now he is dead and the police will be called in and I shall be suspected of having had a hand in it. Oh yes, I am sure I shall. But you don't think so, gentlemen. Surely you don't think it was I? Is it likely that I would have brought you here if it were I? Oh, dear! Oh, dear! I know that I shall go mad!

HOLMES: You have no reason for fear, Mr. Sholto. Take my advice and go down to the station to report the matter to the police. Offer to assist them in every way. We shall wait here until you return.

SHOLTO: Yes. Yes. I will.

(Thaddeus leaves)

HOLMES: Now, Watson, we have some time to ourselves. Let us make good use of it. My case is almost complete but we must not err on the side of overconfidence. Simple as the case seems now, there may be something deeper underlying it.

WATSON: Simple!?

HOLMES: Surely. Now to work. In the first place, how did these folk come and go? The door? No, it has been locked from the inside since last night.

WATSON: The window?

(Holmes carries the lantern over to the window and inspects it carefully.)

HOLMES: Window is latched but snibbed on the inner side. Framework is solid. (Opening and looking out) No water pipe near and we're three stories up. Roof quite out of reach. And yet a man has mounted by the window. Here is a footprint in the dust on the sill. (Moving across the room while inspecting the ground) And here upon the floor is a drag mark and a circular muddy mark and here again and here again by the table. See here, Watson! This is really a very pretty demonstration.

(Watson joins Holmes to look at the mark.)

WATSON: That is not a footmark.

HOLMES: It is something much more valuable to us. It is the impression of a wooden crutch.

WATSON: It is the lame man.

HOLMES: Quite so. But there has been someone else – a very able and efficient ally. Could you scale that wall, Doctor? *(Gesturing out the window)*

WATSON: *(Looking out the window)* It is absolutely impossible.

HOLMES: Without aid it is so. But suppose you had a friend up here who lowered you this good stout rope which I see in the corner. Then, I think, you might swarm up, lame leg and all. You could depart in the same fashion and your ally could pull up the rope, latch the window and get away in the way he originally came. It may be mentioned that our climber was not a professional sailor. His hands were far from horny. See here blood marks on the rope from which I gather he slipped down the rope with such velocity that he took skin off his hands.

WATSON: That is all very well, but the thing becomes even more unintelligible than ever. How about this mysterious ally? How came he into the room? The door is locked; the window inaccessible. How then?

HOLMES: *(Shaking his head)* You will not apply my precept? When you have eliminated the impossible, whatever remains, however improbable, must be the truth. We know that he did not come through the door or the window. We also know that he could not still be in the room as there is no concealment possible. Where, then did he come?

WATSON: He came through the hole in the roof!

HOLMES: Of course he did. He must have done so. If you will be so kind as to hold the lamp for me, we shall now extend our researches to the room above – the secret room where the treasure was found.

(Holmes and Watson enter the dressing room with Watson in the doorway and Holmes out of sight.)

HOLMES: *(Calling from inside)* Here you are, you see. There is a trapdoor which leads out onto the roof. This then, is the way by which Number One entered. Come here and look at these footprints.

(Watson disappears into the dressing room)

WATSON: Holmes, a child has done this horrid thing. These footprints are scarcely half the size of an ordinary man.

HOLMES: There is nothing more to be learned here. Let us go down. *(Entering the room)* I must admit, I was staggered for a moment but the thing is quite natural. My memory failed me or I should have been able to foretell it.

WATSON: What is your theory then, as to those footmarks?

HOLMES: My dear, Watson, try a little analysis yourself. You know my methods. Apply them and it will be instructive to compare results.

WATSON: I cannot conceive anything which will cover the facts.

HOLMES: It will be clear enough to you soon. I think that there is nothing else of importance here but I will look.

(Holmes finds a cracked carboy with the chemical equipment and stoops to inspect it carefully)

We are in luck. Number One has had the misfortune to tread in creosote. You can see the outline of the edge of his small foot here at the side of this evil smelling mess. The carboy has cracked and the stuff has leaked out.

WATSON: What then?

HOLMES: Why, we have got him. That's all. I know a dog that would follow that scent to the world's end. *(Looking out the window)* Hallo! Here are the accredited representatives of the law so the auxiliary forces may beat a retreat.

(Jones enters with Thaddeus guarded by Constable Murcher.)

JONES: Here's a business! Here's a pretty business. But who are all these? Why the house seems to be as full as a rabbit-warren!

HOLMES: I think you must recollect me, Mr. Abernathy Jones.

JONES: Why, of course I do. It's Mr. Sherlock Holmes, the theorist. Remember you? I'll never forget how you lectured us all on causes and inferences and effects in the Bishopgate jewel case. It's true you set us on the right track, but you'll own now that it was more by good luck than good guidance.

HOLMES: It was a piece of very simple reasoning.

JONES: Oh, come, now, come! Never be ashamed to own up. But what is all this? Bad business! Bad business! Stern facts here – no room for theories. How lucky that I happened to be out at Norwood over another case. What d'you think the man died of?

HOLMES: Oh this is hardly a case for me to theorize over.

JONES: No, no. Still, we can't deny that you hit the nail on the head sometimes. Dear me! Door locked, I understand. Jewels worth a fortune missing. How was the window?

HOLMES: Fastened but there are steps on the sill.

JONES: Well, well, if it was fastened the steps could have nothing to do with the matter. That's common sense. Man might have died in a fit but the jewels are missing. Ha! I have a theory. These flashes come upon me at times. Constable, please escort Mr. Sholto outside.

MURCHER: Yes sir.

(They leave)

What do you think of this, Holmes? Sholto was, on his own confessions, with his brother last night. The brother died in a fit and Sholto walked off with the treasure.

HOLMES: On which the dead man very considerately got up and locked the door on the inside.

JONES: Hum! There's a flaw there. Let us apply common sense to the matter. This Thaddeus Sholto was with his brother. There was a quarrel; so much we know. The brother is dead and the jewels are gone. So much we also know. No one saw the brother after Thaddeus left him. Thaddeus is evidently in a most disturbed state of mind. His appearance is – well, not attractive. You see that I am weaving my web round Thaddeus. The net begins to close upon him.

HOLMES: You are not quite in possession of the facts yet. This splinter of wood, which I have every reason to believe is poisoned, was in the man's neck; this card, inscribed as you see, was pinned to his back and on the table lay this rather curious stone headed instrument. How does all that fit your theory?

JONES: Confirms it in every respect. House is full of Indian curiosities. Thaddeus brought this up and if the thorn is poisonous Thaddeus may as well have made murderous use of it as anyone else. The card is some hocus-pocus – a blind to throw us off the track, as like not. The only question is how did he depart?

(Jones searches around and ends up in the dressing room)

Ah, of course, here is a hole in the roof. Aha!

HOLMES: He can find some things. He has occasional glimmerings of reason.

JONES: *(Entering)* You see! Facts are better than theories after all. My view of the case is confirmed. There is a trapdoor communicating with the roof and it is partly opened.

HOLMES: It was I who opened it.

JONES: Oh, indeed. You did notice it then? Well, whoever noticed it, it shows how our gentleman got away. Constable Murcher!

MURCHER: *(From passage)* Yes, sir?

JONES: Bring Mr. Sholto back in.

MURCHER: Right away, Inspector.

(Murcher re-enters with Thaddeus)

JONES: Mr. Sholto, it is my duty to inform you that anything which you may say will be used against you. I arrest you in the Queen's name for the death of your brother.

SHOLTO: There now! Didn't I tell you?

HOLMES: Don't trouble yourself about it, Mr. Sholto. I think that I can engage to clear you of the charge.

JONES: Don't promise too much, Mr. Theorist.

HOLMES: Not only will I clear him, Mr. Jones, but I will make you a free present of the name and description of one of the two people who were in this room last night. His name is Jonathan Small. He is a poorly educated man, active but lame, dragging his right foot and using a crutch. He is a middle-aged man and has been a convict. Also, there is a good deal of skin missing from the palm of his hands. The other man…

JONES: Ah! The other man?

HOLMES: The other man is a rather curious person. I hope to be able to introduce you to the pair of them before too long.

JONES: More theories? Constable, escort Mr. Sholto to the wagon. You'll see there's nothing more here than brothers fighting over a treasure. Go home and sleep well, Mr. Holmes.

(Murcher, Thaddeus and Jones exit. Watson begins to follow them out.)

HOLMES: A word with you, Watson. This unexpected occurrence has caused us to lose sight of the original purpose of our journey.

WATSON: I have just been thinking so. It is not right that Miss Morstan should remain in this stricken house.

HOLMES: No, you must escort her home. She lives in Lower Camberwell so it is not very far. I will wait for you here if you will drive out again. Or perhaps you are too tired?

WATSON: By no means, I don't think I could rest until I know more of this fantastic business. I should like to see the matter through with you.

HOLMES: Your presence will be of great service to me. We shall work the case out independently and leave this fellow Jones to exult over any mare's nest which he may choose to construct. Now, I wish you to go to Number 3 Pinchin Lane, down near Lambeth. The third house on the right is the bird stuffer's; Sherman is his name. Tell him, with my compliments that I want Toby at once. You will bring Toby back with you in the cab.

WATSON: A dog, I suppose.

HOLMES: I would rather have Toby's help than that of the whole detective force of London.

WATSON: I shall bring him then.

HOLMES: And I shall see what I can learn from Mrs. Bernstone and from the Indian Servant. Then I shall study the great Jones' methods and listen to his not too delicate sarcasms.

WATSON: It is one now. I ought to be back by three if I can get a fresh horse.

HOLMES: Then make haste, Watson. The game is afoot.

END OF ACT 1

ACT 2

Scene 1 – Street Outside Mrs. Forrester's Home

(The street outside Mrs. Cecil Forrester's house. The street is dark. Watson and Mary enter.)

MISS MORSTAN: This is the place, Doctor. Thank you for your kindness. It is very late and I'm afraid my emotions are stretched very thin.

WATSON: It was my duty and pleasure, Miss Morstan. I don't know that I would have held up as well in your place. To finally know the fate of your unfortunate father. At least that should give you some comfort.

MISS MORSTAN: If only he had not gone to Major Sholto's, I may have seen him one more time.

(Mary finally breaks down and starts sobbing. Watson wants to console her but hesitates. Finally, he offers his handkerchief from his sleeve.)

You must think me useless.

WATSON: Quite the contrary. You were quite bright and placid by the side of Mrs. Bernstone. She was very upset.

MISS MORSTAN: Can you blame her? She described her master's face to me. I'm happy that it was not I that saw it.

WATSON: I'm sure she is much the better off for your calm face and angelic demeanor. Still, who am I to judge if you have been sorely tried by the adventures of the night, Miss Morstan?

(Mary takes his handkerchief and wipes her tears and rests her head upon his shoulder as Watson does his best to be comforting. Mrs. Forrester enters from the house.)

MRS FORRESTER: Mary, my dear, *(embracing her)* I was getting so worried about you. It's nearly two o'clock. Everyone else is abed but I couldn't sleep until I knew you were safe.

MISS MORSTAN: I am safe and home. *(Introducing Watson)* Mrs. Forrester, this is Dr. Watson, the associate of Mr. Sherlock Holmes I was telling you about.

WATSON: A pleasure, madam.

MRS FORRESTER: Oh, Mary, I see what you mean. You are a handsome one, even if you do need to put a little meat on your bones.

WATSON: *(Embarrassed)* Yes, well... I've been ill.

MRS FORRESTER: Back from the war, Mary tells me.

WATSON: Yes, on inactive duty due to my health.

MRS FORRESTER: You look fine to me, Doctor.

MISS MORSTAN: *(Also embarrassed)* The Doctor was just seeing me home. It's been a very eventful night.

MRS FORRESTER: Oh Doctor, you must come in and tell me of all your adventures this evening. Surely it must be peculiar indeed to keep you out till this late hour.

WATSON: I would like nothing more but the importance of my errand prevents me from staying. I shall, however, call and report any progress which we might make.

MRS FORRESTER: I shall hold you to that, Doctor. Come inside dear.

(Mrs. Forrester exits.)

MISS MORSTAN: You must forgive Mrs. Forrester. She has it in her head that I should settle down and start a family of my own.

WATSON: There's nothing wrong with that… if you've found the right man, of course.

MISS MORSTAN: Of course.

WATSON: *(Realizing the implications of what he has said and tripping over his own tongue)* Ah, yes… She obviously cares for you.

MISS MORSTAN: I've no doubt of that. She's been more like the mother I never had.

WATSON: I had forgotten. Forgive me, it must have been hard growing up without either parent.

MISS MORSTAN: It wasn't all bad. I saw Papa whenever he was on leave and I was certainly well cared for.

WATSON: What was he like, the Captain?

MISS MORSTAN: He was very kind, and very dear to me. I never once heard him raise his voice. And yet, I feel as if I never really knew him. He would never tell me stories of his time in the service. If it weren't for his uniform, I might never have known he was a soldier. And you? What of your family?

WATSON: I have no family now. My elder brother was the last and he passed away while I was in Afghanistan.

MISS MORSTAN: It must be lonely.

WATSON: I suppose I have Holmes.

MISS MORSTAN: Mr. Holmes? He seems distant.

WATSON: *(laughing)* He's not so bad. He grows on you after a while.

MISS MORSTAN: I completely understand, Doctor. One learns to make do with the family they have, related or not.

WATSON: You continue to astound me, Miss Morstan. Your strength is admirable.

MISS MORSTAN: Is it merely my strength you admire, Doctor?

WATSON: It is one of many qualities to be admired.

MISS MORSTAN: Do you think Mr. Holmes will be able to find the killer?

WATSON: I don't know. He is possessed with an overabundance of confidence and I hardly know if it is warranted or not. If his confidence is to be believed, he will solve this singular incident and find the killer and the treasure.

MISS MORSTAN: Of course, the treasure. It's a thought that has not yet settled on my mind.

WATSON: Your share will make you immensely wealthy.

(Watson is uncomfortable with the idea that Mary will be wealthy while he is a poor Doctor. His demeanor becomes colder as he contemplates the idea that Mary will be above his station.)

MISS MORSTAN: Yes, there is that. I wouldn't know what to do with that sort of wealth.

WATSON: Establish your own household, no doubt. You would leave Mrs. Forrester's employ, of course.

MISS MORSTAN: Yes, I suppose I would.

WATSON: *(with a little more bile than he really means)* Servants, a nice house in the country. Find yourself a husband befitting your fortune and settle down to start that family you mentioned earlier.

MISS MORSTAN: Has something upset you, Doctor?

WATSON: Not at all. I should be off on my errand. Holmes will be expecting me.

MRS FORRESTER: *(From offstage)* Mary.

MISS MORSTAN: Coming! Of course, Doctor. Goodnight and thank you.

(Mary offers her hand. Again Watson shakes it awkwardly while they look into each other's eyes. It's becoming apparent that Mary too may be smitten but she is confused by Watson's sudden coldness.)

WATSON: Good night, Miss Morstan.

(Mary exits. Watson watches briefly and then turns and hurries off.)

END OF SCENE

Scene 2 – Entrance Gate, Pondicherry Lodge

(Pondicherry Lodge Gate. Holmes is smoking his pipe as Watson and Wiggins enter.)

WIGGINS: Evenin' Mr. 'Olmes.

HOLMES: Wiggins. A bit late for you, is it not?

WIGGINS: Oh no sir. As I understand it, you got some investigatin' to do and I'm your man.

WATSON: I found this one at the bird stuffer's. He insisted he's good with dogs and he should come along. I tried to dissuade him.

HOLMES: Quite all right. Since you're here, I have a task for you. You see that rain barrel against the house with the water pipe?

WIGGINS: Aye.

HOLMES: I want you to scamper up that pipe to the roof. Once on the roof, there is a trap door into a crawlspace and a hole in the ceiling. Drop down into the room and come back down via the house. Think you can do that?

WIGGINS: No problem, sir.

HOLMES: I want you to keep an eye out for anything out of place or unusual. I've already examined the room, so focus on the climb and the roof. I want a full report.

WIGGINS: You can count on me, guv'nor. (Turns to leave)

WATSON: Wiggins…

WIGGINS: Yes sir?

WATSON: Go carefully.

WIGGINS: Most definitely, sir.

(Wiggins leaves towards the house.)

HOLMES: He'll be fine, Doctor. A most capable young man but don't let him hear you say that.

WATSON: His family won't be cross with you for using him?

HOLMES: Mother passed away in childbirth with his youngest brother and his father's a drunkard who's unlikely to know he's even here.

WATSON: I see.

HOLMES: He's a good sort, sharp as a tack and more observant than most. *(whistling)* Toby?

(dog barks offstage)

WATSON: We left him tied outside the gate. We were just coming to get you.

HOLMES: Abernathy Jones has gone. We have had an immense display of energy since you left. He arrested not only friend Thaddeus but the gatekeeper - the housekeeper - the coachman - and the Indian servant. What do you think of it?

WATSON: He certainly casts a wide net.

HOLMES: I tried to tell him he was fishing in the wrong pond but he's far too clever for me. Come over here. I wish you to notice these footmarks. Do you observe anything noteworthy about them?

WATSON: They belong to a child or small woman.

HOLMES: Apart from their size though. Is there nothing else?

WATSON: No, they appear to be much as other footmarks.

HOLMES: Not at all. Look here. This is the print of a right foot in the dust and beside it a print I made with my own naked foot. What is the chief difference?

WATSON: Your toes are all cramped together. The smaller print has each toe distinctly divided.

HOLMES: Quite so. That is the point. Bear that in mind.

WATSON: I shall but I still fail to see what bearing this has on tonight's mystery.

HOLMES: In due time. Over there, against the wall. Smell the edge of the flagstone.

(Watson gets down and takes a whiff of the ground.)

WATSON: There's a strong tarry smell.

HOLMES: That is where he put his foot getting down. If you can trace him, I should think Toby will have no difficulties even with their twenty four hour head start.

(Wiggins enters.)

WATSON: That didn't take long.

WIGGINS: No problem at all. There's good footholds the whole way up.

HOLMES: What did you find?

WIGGINS: Someone else has been climbin' there, sir. It was easy to follow him. Tiles were loosened the whole way along and he dropped this.

(Wiggins hands Holmes a pouch with some beads strung around it. He takes a look then hands it to Watson.)

HOLMES: Did you touch anything in that bag?

WIGGINS: No, sir. I brought it straight away to you.

HOLMES: Just as well you didn't.

WATSON: There's a couple dozen of those poisoned spines in here, Holmes.

HOLMES: They are hellish things. Look out that you don't prick yourself. I'm delighted to have them for the chances are that they are all he has and now there is less fear of you or me finding one in our skin before long. I would sooner face a bullet, myself. Are you game for a six-mile trudge, Watson?

WATSON: Certainly.

HOLMES: Your leg will stand it?

WATSON: Oh, yes.

HOLMES: Then let's be off.

(All exit)

END OF SCENE

Scene 3 – Streets of London

(There is a bench upstage center with a burning street-light beside it. The baying of a hound dog can be heard in the distance getting further away. Wiggins runs in with a leash in his hands. He pauses and then calls back to Holmes and Watson.)

WIGGINS: He went this way, sir.

(Holmes enters, a bit winded from running.)

HOLMES: You run after him. I'll wait here for the Doctor.

WIGGINS: The way has been a rather curious zigzag road, wouldn't you say, Mr. 'Olmes?

HOLMES: Probably with the idea of escaping observation. Now get along before Toby gets too far ahead of us.

WIGGINS: Aye. I'll catch him up and wait for you on the east side of the Oval.

(Wiggins runs off as Watson comes limping in out of breath and obviously in pain.)

WATSON: Sorry for keeping you back, Holmes.

HOLMES: Not at all, Doctor. We'll walk at your pace; Wiggins will see to Toby. We're definitely on the right trail. Look here, the print of the lame-legged man's hand. You see the slight smudge of blood.

WATSON: I confess that I had my doubts.

HOLMES: Do not imagine that I depend for my success in this case upon the mere chance of one of these fellows having put his foot in creosote. I have knowledge now that would allow me to trace them in different ways. This, however, is the readiest and since fortune has put it in our hands, I should be culpable if I neglected it. It has, however, prevented the case from becoming the pretty little intellectual problem which it at one time promised to be. There might have been some credit to be gained out of it but for this too palpable clue.

WATSON: There is credit, and to spare. I assure you, Holmes, that I marvel at the means which you obtain your results. How, for example could you describe with such confidence the lame-legged man?

HOLMES: Pshaw, my dear boy! It was simplicity itself. I don't wish to be theatrical. Two officers who are in command of a convict guard learn an important secret as to buried treasure. A map is drawn for them by an Englishman named Jonathan Small. You remember that we saw the name upon the chart in Captain Morstan's possession. He had signed it in behalf of himself and his associates, the sign of four, as he somewhat dramatically called it. Aided by the chart, the officers get the treasure and bring it to England.

WATSON: Why did not Jonathan Small get the treasure himself?

HOLMES: The answer is obvious. The chart is dated at a time when Morstan was brought into close association with convicts. Jonathan Small did not get the treasure because he and his associates were themselves convicts and could not get away.

WATSON: But this is mere speculation.

HOLMES: It is more than that. It is the only hypothesis which covers the facts. Let's see how it fits with the sequel. Major Sholto remains at peace for some years, happy to be in possession of the treasure. Then he receives a letter from India which gives him a great fright. What was that?

WATSON: A letter to say that the men whom he had wronged had been set free.

HOLMES: Or escaped. That is much more likely for he would have known the term of their imprisonment. What does he do then?

WATSON: Guards himself against a lame man.

HOLMES: A white man, mark you, for he mistakes a white tradesman for him and actually fires a pistol at him. Now, only one white man's name is on the chart.

WATSON: Jonathan Small.

HOLMES: Precisely, the others are Hindus or Mohammedans. Therefore we may say with confidence that the lame man is Jonathan Small. Does the reasoning strike you as being faulty?

WATSON: No. It is clear and concise.

HOLMES: Well then, let us place ourselves in the place of Jonathan Small. He comes to England with the double idea of regaining what he regards as rightfully his and of having revenge upon the man who had wronged him. Small could not find out where the treasure was hid so he bides his time.

WATSON: But then the Major fell ill and was on his deathbed.

HOLMES: Indeed, Watson. What would you do in Small's place?

WATSON: Rush to Norwood, lest the secret of the treasure die with him. He was only deterred from entering the room by the presence of his two sons. Later, he enters the room, searches his private papers for some memorandum relating to the treasure and finally leaves a memento of his visit, the card reading "The Sign of Four."

HOLMES: Now you are getting the hang of it, Doctor. No doubt he had planned to confront him and had the card prepared beforehand that, should he slay the Major, he would leave a record that this was not a common murder but an act of justice. Do you follow all of this?

WATSON: Very clearly.

HOLMES: Now what could Jonathan Small do? He could only continue to keep watch in the hopes that the treasure is found. Then comes the discovery. Jonathan, with his lame leg, is utterly unable to reach Bartholomew Sholto's room. He takes with him a rather curious associate who gets over this difficulty but dips his naked foot into creosote, whence come Toby, and a six mile limp for a half-pay officer with a damaged tendo Achilles.

WATSON: But it was the associate and not Small who committed the crime.

HOLMES: Quite so. And rather to Small's disgust to judge from the way he stamped about when he got into the room. He held no grudge against Bartholomew Sholto and did not wish to put his head in a halter. That is the train of events as far as I can decipher them.

WATSON: As to his personal appearance?

HOLMES: He must be middle aged and his height is readily calculated from the length of his stride and we know he was bearded, the hairiness was the one point which impressed itself upon Thaddeus Sholto.

WATSON: The associate?

HOLMES: Ah, well, there is no great mystery in that. But you will know all about it soon enough. Did you bring your bull pup?

WATSON: I'm afraid not. It's in my desk. I have my stick.

(Holmes takes his pistol from his pocket, checks the chamber and verifies it is loaded then sticks it back in his pocket. Wiggins enters.)

HOLMES: I have mine. It is just possible that we may need something of the sort if we get to their lair. Jonathan I shall leave to you but if the other turns nasty I shall shoot him dead.

WIGGINS: Mr. 'Olmes, sir.

HOLMES: I thought you were going to wait for us at the Oval?

WIGGINS: I was sir but when I caught up to Toby he was at the end of Broad Street where it runs right down to the water where there was a small wooden wharf. He was just standin' there whinin', looking out on the dark water beyond.

HOLMES: Well, we are out of luck, then. They have taken to a boat.

WIGGINS: There's a small brick house there, sir. Owner is a Cap'n Smith. He hires a steam launch by the hour. Most likely they took that.

HOLMES: Wiggins, you have performed admirably. Collect Toby and take him back to the birdstuffer's. Watson and I shall have a look at this wharf.

WIGGINS: Aye sir.

HOLMES: What does that watch of yours tell you, Watson?

WATSON: *(Looking at watch)* It's just after seven, Holmes.

HOLMES: Come, Doctor. Let us see what this Captain Smith has to say.

END OF SCENE

Scene 4 – Wharf on Broad Street

(On the Broad Street near the wharf, outside of Mordecai Smith's house. Holmes and Watson enter.)

WATSON: *(reading sign)* Mordecai Smith. Boats to hire by the hour or day.

HOLMES: This looks bad. These fellows are sharper than I expected. They seem to have covered their tracks. There has, I fear, been pre-concerted management here.

(The door comes open and a young, dirty, lad comes running out, followed by a woman, Mrs. Smith, with a sponge in her hand.)

MRS SMITH: You come back and be washed, Jack. Come back you young imp, for if your father comes home and finds you like that he'll let us hear of it.

HOLMES: Dear little chap! What a rosy cheeked young rascal. Now Jack, is there anything you would like?

JACK: I'd like a shillin'.

HOLMES: Nothing you would like better?

JACK: I'd like two shillin' better.

HOLMES: Here you are, then. Catch!

(Jack takes his coins and runs off gleefully.)

A fine child, Mrs. Smith.

MRS SMITH: Lor' bless you, sir, he is that, and forward. He gets a'most too much for me to manage, 'specially when my man is away days at a time.

HOLMES: Away is he? I am sorry for that, for I wanted to speak to Mr. Smith.

MRS SMITH: He's been away since yesterday mornin', sir, and, truth to tell, I am beginnin' to feel frightened about him. But if it was about a boat, sir, maybe I could serve as well.

HOLMES: I wanted to hire his steam launch.

MRS SMITH: Why, bless you, sir, it is the steam launch that he has gone. That's what puzzles me, for I know there ain't more coals in her than would take her to about Woolwhich and back. If he's been away in the barge I'd ha' thought nothin'; for many a time a job has taken him as far as Gravesend, and then if there was much doin' there might stay over. But what good is a steam launch without coals?

WATSON: He might have bought some at a wharf down the river.

MRS SMITH: He might, sir, but it weren't his way. Many a time I've heard him call out at the prices they charge for a few odd bags. Besides, I don't like that lame man wi' his ugly face and outlandish talk. What did he want always knockin' about here for?

HOLMES: A lame man?

MRS SMITH: Yes sir, a brown, monkey faced chap that's called more'n once for my old man. It was him that roused him up in the night and, what's more, my man knew he was comin', for he had the steam up in the launch. I tell you straight, sir, I don't feel easy in my mind about it.

HOLMES: But, my dear Mrs. Smith, you are frightening yourself about nothing. How could you possibly tell that it was the lame man who came in the night? I don't understand how you can be so sure.

MRS SMITH: His voice, sir. I knew his voice, which is kind o' thick and foggy. He tapped at the winder, about midnight it would be. 'Show a leg, matey,' says he: 'time to turn out guard.' My old man woke up Jim –

that's my eldest – and away they went without so much as a word to me. I could hear his crutch clackin' on the stones.

HOLMES: And was the lame-legged man alone?

MRS SMITH: Couldn't say, I am sure. I didn't hear no one else.

HOLMES: I am sorry, Mrs. Smith, for I wanted a steam launch, and I have heard good reports of the – Let me see, what is her name?

MRS SMITH: The Aurora, sir.

HOLMES: Ah! She's not that old green launch with a yellow line, very broad in the beam?

MRS SMITH: No indeed. She's as trim a little thing as any on the river. She's been fresh painted, black with two red streaks.

HOLMES: Thanks. I hope that you will hear soon from Mr. Smith. I am going down the river and if I should see anything of the Aurora, I shall let him know that you are uneasy. A black funnel, you say?

MRS SMITH: No, sir. Black with a white band.

HOLMES: Ah, of course. It was the sides which were black. Good morning, Mrs. Smith.

(Mrs. Smith exits)

HOLMES: The main thing with people of that sort is never to let them think that their information can be of the slightest importance to you. If they do, they will instantly shut up like an oyster. If you listen to them under protest, as it were, you are very likely to get what you want.

WATSON: Our course now seems pretty clear.

HOLMES: What would you do then?

WATSON: I would engage a launch and go down the river on the track of the Aurora.

HOLMES: My dear fellow, it would be a colossal task. She may have touched at any wharf on either side of the stream between here and Greenwich. Below the bridge there is a perfect labyrinth of landing-places for miles. It would take you days and days to exhaust them if you set about it alone.

WATSON: Employ the police, then.

HOLMES: No. I shall probably call Abernathy Jones in the last moment. He is not a bad fellow and I should not like to do anything which would injure him professionally. But I have a fancy for working it out myself now that we have gone so far.

WATSON: Could we advertise, then, asking for information from wharfingers?

HOLMES: Worse and worse! Our men would know that the chase was hot at their heels and they would be off out of the country. Jones' energy will be of use to us there, for his view of the case is sure to push itself into the daily press and the runaways will think that everyone is off on the wrong scent.

WATSON: What are we to do then?

HOLMES: Take a hansom, drive home, have some breakfast and get an hour's sleep. It is quite on the cards that we might be afoot again tonight.

END OF SCENE

Scene 5 – 221 B Baker Street

(Holmes is in a robe, seated at the table where breakfast is laid. He is pouring coffee as Watson enters, also robed.)

HOLMES: Did you have a good sleep?

WATSON: I am perfectly fresh now and quite ready for another night's outing.

HOLMES: (Pointing to the open newspaper) Take a look at this. The energetic Jones and the ubiquitous reporter have fixed it between them. But you have had enough of the case. Better have your ham and eggs first.

WATSON: *(Picking up the paper and reading)*

"Mysterious Business at Upper Norwood. About twelve o'clock last night Mr. Bartholomew Sholto of Pondicherry Lodge, Upper Norwood, was found dead in his room under circumstances which point to foul play. No actual traces of violence were found but a valuable collection of Indian gems has been carried off. The discovery was made by Mr. Sherlock Holmes and Dr. John Watson who had called at the house with Mr. Thaddeus Sholto, brother of the deceased. By a singular piece of good fortune, Mr. Abernathy Jones, the well-known member of the detective police force, happened to be at the Norwood Police station and was on the grounds within a half an hour of the first alarm. His trained and experienced faculties were at once directed towards detection of the criminals, with the gratifying result that the brother, Thaddeus Sholto, has already been arrested, together with the housekeeper, Mrs. Bernstone, an Indian butler named Lal Rao and a porter named McMurdo."

HOLMES: Isn't it gorgeous! What do you think of it?

WATSON: I think we have had a close shave ourselves of being arrested for the crime.

HOLMES: So do I. I wouldn't answer for our safety now if he should happen to have another of his attacks of energy.

(Bell rings)

MRS HUDSON: *(From offstage)* Oh, not you lot.

WATSON: By heavens, Holmes. I believe they are really after us.

HOLMES: No, it's not quite so bad as that. It's the unofficial force – the Baker Street Irregulars.

(Wiggins enters with Stephenson. Mrs. Hudson follows them on with an annoyed demeanor.)

MRS HUDSON: Mr. Holmes, sir. I can't be havin' this lot of urchins bustin' in here and muddying up my floors. It's bad enough I have to keep after the two of you.

HOLMES: I will take care of it, Mrs. Hudson.

MRS HUDSON: *(to herself as she leaves)* You would think this was Paddington Station and not a respectable residence.

HOLMES: Wiggins, Stephenson.

WIGGINS: Got your message sir and brought 'em on sharp.

HOLMES: Where are the rest of the boys?

WIGGINS: All down on the street. Mrs. Hudson refused to let us all up.

HOLMES: Just as well. In the future, they can report to you, Wiggins, and you to me. In the interest of keeping the peace, we cannot have the house invaded in this way.

WIGGINS: Understood, Mr. 'Olmes. We'll keep the troops on the outside.

HOLMES: You remember Mr. Mordecai Smith from last evening?

WIGGINS: The one with the launch down on Broad Street?

HOLMES: That's the man. I want to find the whereabouts of his steam launch called the Aurora, black with two red streaks, funnel black with a white band. She is down the river somewhere. I want one boy to be at Mordecai Smith's landing to say if the boat comes back. You must divide it among yourselves and do both banks thoroughly. Let me know the moment you have news. Is that all clear?

WIGGINS: Yes, guv'nor.

STEPHENSON: Yes, guv'nor.

HOLMES: The old scale of pay, and a guinea to the boy who finds the boat. Here's a day in advance. Now off you go! *(to Watson)* If the launch is above water they will find her. *(Lighting his pipe)* They can go everywhere, see everything, overhear everyone. I expect to hear before evening that they have spotted her. In the meanwhile, we can do nothing but await the results.

WATSON: Are you going to bed, Holmes?

HOLMES: No. I am not tired. I have a curious constitution. I never remember feeling tired by work but idleness exhausts me completely. I am going to smoke and think over this queer business. Lame-legged men are not so common but this other man must, I should think, be absolutely unique.

WATSON: That other man again.

HOLMES: I have no wish to make a mystery of him to you, anyway. But you must have formed your own opinion. Now, do consider the data. Diminutive footmarks, toes never fettered by boots, naked feet, stone-headed wooden mace, great agility, small poisoned thorns. What do you make of all this?

WATSON: A savage! Perhaps one of those Indians who were the associates of Jonathan Small.

HOLMES: Hardly that. When I first saw the strange weapons, I was inclined to think so but then I saw the character of the footmarks. The Hindu has long and thin feet and the Mohammadan has the great toe separated from the rest because a thong is commonly passed between. These little thorns too are from a blow-pipe. Now then, where are we to find our savage?

WATSON: South America?

HOLMES: *(Taking a book from a shelf and reading)*

"Andaman Islands, situated 340 miles to the north of Sumatra in the Bay of Bengal."

Hum! Hum! What's all this? Moist climate, coral reefs, sharks, Port Blair, convict barracks... Ah, here we are!

"The aborigines of the Andaman Islands may perhaps claim the distinction of being the smallest race upon this earth. They are a fierce, morose and intractable people, though capable of forming most devoted friendships when their confidence has once been gained."

Mark that Watson. Now listen to this.

"They are naturally hideous, misshapen heads and distorted features. Their feet and hands, however, are remarkably small. They have always been a horror to shipwrecked crews, braining the survivors with their stone-headed clubs or shooting them with their poisoned darts. These massacres are invariably concluded with a cannibal feast."

Nice amiable people, Watson! If this fellow had been left to his own devices, this affair may have taken a more ghastly turn. I fancy that, even as it is, Jonathan Small would give a good deal not to have employed him.

WATSON: But how came he to have so singular a companion?

HOLMES: That is more than I can tell. Since we know Small came from the Andamans, it is not so very wonderful that this islander should be with him. No doubt we shall know all about it in time.

WATSON: Can I do anything?

HOLMES: No, we can do nothing, only wait. You can do what you will but I must be on guard.

WATSON: Then I shall run over to Camberwell and call upon Mrs. Cecil Forrester. She asked me to earlier.

HOLMES: On Mrs. Cecil Forrester? (with an amused knowing look)

WATSON: Well, of course on Miss Morstan too. They were anxious to hear what happened.

HOLMES: I would not tell them too much. Women are never to be trusted – not the best of them.

(Watson is obviously taken aback by Holmes' mistrust of women. He starts as if to say something then thinks better of it and lets it go.)

WATSON: I shall be back in an hour or two.

END OF SCENE

Scene 6 – 221 B Baker Street

(It is several days later. There are books all over the table where Holmes usually sits. His pipe and violin are both laid out, discarded. Mrs. Hudson is scurrying around the room, straightening up as best she can when Watson enters.)

WATSON: Good morning Mrs. Hudson. I suppose Mr. Holmes has gone out.

MRS HUDSON: No sir. He has gone to his room, sir. Do you know, sir, *(lowering her voice to a whisper)* I am afraid for his health.

WATSON: Why so, Mrs. Hudson?

MRS HUDSON: Well, he's that strange, sir. For three days now, ever since you discovered that body in Norwood, he has been walking up and down, up and down, and up and down until I was weary of his footstep. Then I heard him talking to himself and muttering and every time the bell rang out he came on the stair head with 'What is that Mrs. Hudson?' And now he has slammed off to his room. I hope he's not going to be ill, sir. I ventured to say something to him about cooling medicine but he turned on me, sir, with such a look that I don't know how ever I got out of the room.

WATSON: I don't think that you have any cause to be uneasy, Mrs. Hudson. He has some small matter on his mind that makes him restless.

HOLMES: *(From offstage)* Watson, is that you?

MRS HUDSON: I'll leave him to you, then, Doctor.

(Mrs. Hudson exits as Holmes enters from his room looking worn and haggard.)

WATSON: You are knocking yourself up, old man. I heard you marching about in the night.

HOLMES: I could not sleep. This infernal problem is consuming me. It is too much to be balked by so petty an obstacle when all else has been overcome.

WATSON: No news then.

HOLMES: Wiggins has just been up to report. He says no trace can be found of the launch and the boys have been searching for three days. I must confess I am surprised and disappointed. It is a provoking check for every hour is of importance. I shall come to the conclusion soon that they have scuttled the craft.

WATSON: Or that Mrs. Smith has put us on the wrong scent.

HOLMES: No, I think that may be dismissed. I have made inquiries and there is a launch of that description.

WATSON: Could it have gone up the river?

HOLMES: I have considered that possibility too and there is a search party who will work as far as Richmond.

WATSON: Have you seen any of today's newspapers?

HOLMES: Not as of yet.

WATSON: There are articles in most of them upon the Norwood tragedy. They all appear to be rather hostile to the unfortunate Thaddeus Sholto. There's no new news, only that they were holding an inquest this morning.

(Holmes retrieves his coat and hat.)

HOLMES: I am off down the river, Watson. I have been turning it over in my mind and I can see only one way out of it. It is worth trying, at all events.

WATSON: Surely I can come with you, then?

HOLMES: No. You can be much more useful if you will remain here as my representative. I am loath to go, for it is quite on the cards that some message may come during the day, though Wiggins was despondent about it. I want you to open all notes and telegrams and to act on your own judgment if any news should come. Can I rely on you?

WATSON: Most certainly.

HOLMES: I am afraid that you will not be able to wire for me for I can hardly tell yet where I may find myself. With luck, I may not be gone so very long.

WATSON: Good luck, Holmes.

HOLMES: And to you, Doctor.

END OF SCENE

Scene 7 – 221 B Baker Street

(It is several hours later. Watson is seated at the table reading the newspaper. The bell rings and we can hear Jones from offstage.)

JONES: *(From offstage)* I must speak with Mr. Sherlock Holmes.

(Mrs. Hudson and Jones enter. Jones is not as brusque as before and is rather downcast with a meek and apologetic bearing.)

MRS HUDSON: Doctor Watson, sir. The detective insisted he talk to someone.

(Mrs. Hudson exits.)

JONES: Good-day, sir, good-day. Mr. Sherlock Holmes is out, I understand.

WATSON: Yes, he left early this morning and has been gone about eight hours. I cannot be sure when he will be back. But perhaps you would care to wait. Take a chair and try one of these cigars.

JONES: Thank you, I don't mind if I do.

WATSON: A whisky and soda?

JONES: Well, half a glass. It is very hot for the time of year and I have had a good deal to worry and try me. You know my theory about this Norwood case?

(Watson pours Jones a drink.)

WATSON: I remember that you expressed one.

JONES: Well, I have been obliged to reconsider it. I had my net drawn tightly around Mr. Sholto, sir, when pop he went through a hole in the middle of it. He was able to prove an alibi which could not be shaken. From the time that he left his brother's room he was never out of the sight of someone or other. So it could not be he who climbed over roofs and through trapdoors. It is a very dark case and my professional credit is at stake. I should be very glad of a little assistance.

WATSON: We all need help sometimes.

JONES: Your friend, Mr. Sherlock Holmes, is a wonderful man, sir. He's a man not to be beat. I have known that young man to go into a good many cases but I never saw the case yet that he could not throw a light upon. He is irregular in his methods but I think he would have made a most promising officer and I don't care who knows it. I have had a wire from him this afternoon but which I understand he has got a clue to this Sholto business. Here is his message. It was dated from Poplar at twelve o'clock.

"Go to Baker Street at once, If I have not returned, wait for me. I am close on the track of the Sholto gang. You can come with us tonight if you want to be in at the finish."

WATSON: This sounds well. He has evidently picked up the scent again.

JONES: Ah, then he has been at fault too. Even the best of us are thrown off sometimes.

(From offstage we hear a door open and a man breathing hard as though the climb up the stairs was too hard for him. Holmes enters with Mrs. Hudson. He dressed as an elderly sailor with a big beard, old pea-coat using an old oaken cudgel for support, wheezing and coughing. Holmes continues to cough intermittently throughout the conversation.)

MRS HUDSON: Doctor, this *(gives Holmes a disdainful look)* gentleman here insists on seeing someone. He says it is most urgent.

WATSON: Thank you, Mrs. Hudson. You may go. What is it, my man?

(Mrs. Hudson exits.)

HOLMES: Is Mr. Sherlock Holmes here?

WATSON: No, but I am acting for him. You can tell me any message you have for him.

HOLMES: It was to him himself I was to tell it.

WATSON: But I tell you that I am acting for him. Was it about Mordecai Smith's boat?

HOLMES: Yes. I knows well where it is. An' I knows where the men he is after are. An' I knows where the treasure is. I knows all about it.

WATSON: Then tell me and I shall let him know.

HOLMES: It was to him I was to tell it.

WATSON: Well, you must wait for him.

HOLMES: *(coughing in Watson's face and backing him across the room)* No, no. I ain't goin' to lose a whole day to please no one. If Mr. Holmes ain't here, then Mr. Holmes must find it all out for himself. I don't care about the look of either of you, and I won't tell a word.

(Holmes shuffles towards the door but Jones cuts him off.)

JONES: Wait a bit, my friend. You have important information and you must not walk off. We shall keep you, whether or not you like it, until our friend returns.

HOLMES: Pretty sort o' treatment this! I come here to see a gentleman and you two, who I never saw in my life, seize and treat me in this fashion!

WATSON: You will be none the worse. We shall recompense you for the loss of your time. Sit over here on the sofa and you will not have to wait long.

(Holmes takes a seat and Jones and Watson return to their cigars and drink.)

JONES: Do you think he will be much longer, Doctor?

WATSON: Hard to say. He hasn't left me any means to contact him.

HOLMES: *(In his own voice whipping off the wig)* I think that you might offer me a drink too.

WATSON: Holmes. But the old man.

HOLMES: Here is the old man – wig, whiskers, eyebrows and all. I thought my disguise was pretty good, but I hardly expected that it would stand that test.

JONES: Ah, you rogue! You would have made an actor and a rare one. You had the proper workhouse cough and those weak legs of yours are worth ten pound a week. I thought I knew the glint in your eye, though.

HOLMES: I have been working in that get-up all day. You see, a good many of the criminal classes begin to know me: so I can only go on the war path under some simple disguises like this. You got my wire?

JONES: Yes, that was what brought me here.

HOLMES: How has your case prospered?

JONES: It has all come to nothing. I have had to release three of my prisoners and there is no evidence against the other two.

HOLMES: Never mind, we shall give you two others in place of them. You are welcome to the official credit but you must act on the lines that I point out. Is that agreed?

JONES: Entirely, if you will help me to the men.

HOLMES: Well, then, in the first place I shall want a fast police boat – a steam launch – to be at the Westminster Stairs at seven o'clock.

JONES: That is easily managed. There is always one about there.

HOLMES: Then I shall want two staunch men in case of resistance.

JONES: There will be two or three in the boat. What else?

HOLMES: When we secure the men we shall get the treasure. I think that it would be a pleasure to my friend here to show the box to the young lady to whom half of it rightfully belongs. Let her be the first to open it. Eh, Watson?

(The thought of Mary with the treasure and out of his reach does not delight Watson. He is less than enthusiastic.)

WATSON: It would be a great pleasure to me.

JONES: Rather irregular. However, the whole thing is irregular and I suppose we must wink at it. Afterwards, it must be handed over to the authorities until after the official investigation.

HOLMES: Certainly. Also, I would like to speak to Jonathan Small to work out the last details of my case.

JONES: Well, you are the master of the situation. I have had no proof yet of the existence of this Jonathan Small. If you catch him, I don't see how I can refuse you an interview.

HOLMES: That is understood then?

JONES: Perfectly. Is there anything else?

HOLMES: Only that I insist upon you dining with us. It will be ready in half an hour. I have oysters and a brace of grouse with something a little choice in white wines – Watson, you have never yet recognized my merits as a housekeeper.

END OF SCENE

Scene 8 – Upon the River Thames

(The police launch is stage left heading right while the Aurora is stage right. The lights come up only on the police launch. Holmes, Watson and Jones are on the foredeck while Pollock and Murcher are in the wheelhouse.)

HOLMES: Captain, is there anything to mark this as a police boat?

POLLOCK: Yes, that green lamp at the side.

HOLMES: Then take if off.

MURCHER: Yes, sir.

(Murcher takes down the lamp)

JONES: Where to?

HOLMES: To the tower. Stop opposite Jacobson's Yard.

WATSON: This is a quick launch, Holmes. We ought to be able to catch anything on the river.

POLLOCK: Well hardly that. But there are not many launches to beat us.

HOLMES: We shall have to catch the Aurora and she has a reputation for being a clipper. I will tell you how the land lies, Watson. You recollect how annoyed I was at being baulked at so small a thing?

WATSON: Yes.

HOLMES: I asked myself, if I were in Small's shoes, where could I conceal the launch and yet have her on hand at a moment's notice. I might hand the launch over to a repairer with directions to make a trifling change. She would then be removed to his shed or yard and so be effectually concealed while at the same time I could have her at a short notice.

WATSON: That seems simple enough.

HOLMES: It is the simple things that are liable to be overlooked. I inquired all down the river. I drew a blank at the first fifteen but at the sixteenth, Jacobson's, I found the Aurora and the missing owner. He was rather worse for liquor. He bellowed that he wanted it at eight o'clock sharp before he wandered off to an alehouse. I grabbed one of my boys and stationed him as a sentry. He is to wave his handkerchief when they start.

JONES: You've planned it all very neatly. But if the affair were in my hands I should have had a body of police in Jacobson's Yard and arrested them when they came down.

HOLMES: Which would have been never. This Small is a pretty shrewd fellow.

WATSON: But you might have stuck to Smith and so been led to their hiding place.

HOLMES: In that case, I should have wasted my day. I think it is a hundred to one against Smith knowing where they live. As long as he has liquor and good pay, why should he ask questions?

POLLOCK: We're coming up on Jacobson's Yard, sir.

(Holmes takes out binoculars and looks through them. Stephenson is off to the side with a handkerchief, waiting for the Aurora.)

HOLMES: I see my sentry at his post but no sign of a handkerchief.

JONES: Suppose we go downstream a short way and lie in wait for them?

HOLMES: It is certainly ten to one that they go downstream but we can't take anything for granted.

(Stephenson waves his handkerchief.)

POLLOCK: Sir, a white flutter over yonder.

WATSON: Yes, it is your boy. I can see him plainly.

(Lights come up on the Aurora. Smith is at the rudder while Small and Tonga are amidships. They notice the police launch.)

HOLMES: And there is the Aurora and going like the devil. Full speed engineer. Make after that launch with the yellow light. By heaven, I shall never forgive myself if she proves to have the heels of us!

(The opposite side of the stage lights up. It is the Aurora with Mordecai Smith manning the rudder and Jonathan Small and Tonga on the deck.)

POLLOCK: She is very fast. I doubt we shall catch her.

HOLMES: We must catch her. Heap it on stokers! Make her do all she can! If we burn the boat we must have them!

JONES: I think we gain a little.

WATSON: I am sure of it. We shall be up with her in a very few minutes.

JONES: Watch out for that barge.

(The passengers and crew of the police launch are thrown aside as Pollock veers to avoid the barge. Fog horns and bells ring.)

WATSON: Blast! She's gotten ahead of us.

HOLMES: Pile it on, men, pile it on!

SMALL: Smith, blast you! They're gaining on us.

SMITH: *(yelling below decks)* Give her all she's got, Jimmy.

WATSON: Holmes, the savage!

HOLMES: Fire if he raises his hand.

(Tonga raises his blow pipe to his lips. Holmes and Watson fire together. Tonga throws up his hands with a wild scream and then falls overboard.)

JONES: We're nearly upon her.

(Small grabs the rudder out of Smith's hands and turns it roughly to the right. Both men are flung to the deck as the launch changes course.)

SMITH: What are you doing? Are ye mad?

POLLOCK: She's making towards the southern bank.

(Small leaps over the side of the launch, trying to escape inland.)

WATSON: Small has jumped ship, Holmes. He's heading inland.

JONES: Captain, put us to shore there. Quick men, after him.

(Jones and Murcher make for Small who is hobbling across the stage dragging his lame leg. He has lost his crutch and cannot outpace his pursuers. Jones and Murcher easily catch him and drag him back to the Police Launch.)

JONES: Any sign of that savage?

POLLOCK: No, sir. He fell overboard when the shots rang out.

JONES: Most likely at the bottom of the Thames by now.

HOLMES: See here, Watson. We were hardly quick enough with our pistols.

WATSON: It's one of those murderous thorns.

HOLMES: It must have whizzed between us when we fired.

(Murcher boards Aurora and finds an ornate chest with a large lock.)

MURCHER: This would appear to be the treasure, sir.

JONES: Indeed, Constable, take the Aurora and escort her and her crew back to Westminster Stairs.

MURCHER: Aye, sir.

JONES: *(To Small who is laying on the deck)* You, sir, have a lot to answer for. Jonathan Small, I arrest you in the queen's name.

END OF SCENE

Scene 9 – 221 B Baker Street

(Mary is seated when Watson enters with Murcher who is bearing the treasure box. Murcher sets the box down on the table in front of Mary, tips his hat and then exits.)

MISS MORSTAN: I got your wire. Mrs. Hudson let me in.

WATSON: I'm glad you have come.

MISS MORSTAN: What news have you brought me?

WATSON: I have brought you something better than news. I have brought you a fortune.

MISS MORSTAN: *(coolly)* Is that the treasure then?

WATSON: *(with feigned excitement)* Yes, this is the great Agra treasure. Half of it is yours and half is Thaddeus Sholto's. Think of that! There will be few richer young ladies in England. Isn't it glorious?

MISS MORSTAN: If I have it, I owe it to you.

WATSON: No, no, not to me but to Sherlock Holmes. With all the will in the world, I could never have followed up a clue which has taxed even his analytical genius. As it was, we nearly lost it at the last moment.

MISS MORSTAN: Pray sit down and tell me about it, Dr. Watson.

WATSON: Well, since I saw you last, Holmes disguised himself as a wharfinger and discovered the Aurora.

MISS MORSTAN: *(bemused)* He disguised himself?

WATSON: Oh yes, he had a big beard, old ratty clothes and a very convincing stoop. He had Abernathy Jones and I quite fooled.

MISS MORSTAN: I wish I had seen it.

WATSON: Well, we engaged Jones and chased the Aurora down the Thames in a police launch. We barely caught up to her when an Andaman savage, the one who killed Sholto, shot one of his poison thorns at us. It narrowly missed us but he paid the ultimate price and now lies at the bottom of the river.

(At the news that Watson was in danger, Mary grows faint.)

Are you all right, Miss Morstan?

MISS MORSTAN: It is nothing. I am all right again. It was a shock to me to hear that I had placed my friends in such horrible peril.

WATSON: That is all over. It was nothing. I will tell you no more gloomy details. Let us turn to something brighter. There is treasure. What could be brighter than that? I got leave to bring it with me, thinking that it would interest you to be the first to see it.

MISS MORSTAN: It would be of the greatest interest to me. *(She does not seem excited but noticing Watson's puzzled look, changes her tone)* What a pretty box! This is Indian work, I suppose?

WATSON: Yes, it is Benares handi-work.

MISS MORSTAN: The box alone must be of some value. Where is the key?

WATSON: Small threw it into the Thames. We must force it open.

(Watson takes a poker and forces open the lock. They lift the lid and reveal that the treasure has been replaced with coal from the Aurora.)

WATSON: Coal!

MISS MORSTAN: *(Calmly)* The treasure is lost.

WATSON: Thank God!

MISS MORSTAN: Why do you say that?

WATSON: Because you are within my reach again. *(Taking her hand)* Because I love you, Mary, as truly ever a man loved a woman. Because this treasure, these riches, sealed my lips. I did not want you to think that my only interest lay in your riches. Now that they are gone I can tell you how I love you. That is why I said, 'Thank God.'

MISS MORSTAN: *(Drawing him into an embrace)* Then I say 'Thank God' too.

(As Holmes enters, they break their embrace and look sheepishly around. He is accompanied by Small, who is in chains, and Murcher.)

HOLMES: Over there, Constable.

(Holmes gestures to the chair and Murcher drags Small over to the chair and forces him to sit.)

MISS MORSTAN: Who is this then, Doctor?

WATSON: Miss Morstan, this is the Jonathan Small who has caused so much trouble this evening.

SMALL: Morstan? You wouldn't be the Captain's daughter.

MISS MORSTAN: I am.

SMALL: I am right sad for the fate of your father. He was a good man and I had no quarrel with him.

MISS MORSTAN: It is good of you to say so. Doctor, can you please show me out? I do not wish to stay here.

WATSON: Yes, certainly. Excuse us, Holmes. I shall be right back.

MISS MORSTAN: Thank you, Mr. Holmes. I am very glad to have some closure and to know what became of my unfortunate father.

HOLMES: Indeed. Goodbye, Miss Morstan.

(Watson escorts Mary out.)

Well, Jonathan Small, I am sorry that it has come to this.

SMALL: And so am I, sir. I don't believe that I can swing over the job. I give you my word on the book that I never raised a hand against Young Mr. Sholto. It was that little hell-hound, Tonga, who shot one of his cursed darts into him. I had no part in it.

HOLMES: How could you expect so small and weak a man as this Tonga fellow to overpower Mr. Sholto and hold him while you were climbing the rope?

SMALL: You seem to know as much about it as if you were there, sir. Truth is that I had hoped to find the room clear. I knew his habits pretty well and it was the time he usually went down to his supper.

HOLMES: Well, you are under the charge of Mr. Abernathy Jones, of Scotland Yard.

SMALL: That I, who have a fair claim to half a million sterling should spend the first half of my life building breakwaters in the Andamans and am like to spend the other half digging drains at Dartmoor. It was an evil day for me when first had I to do with the Agra treasure.

HOLMES: How did you come into this treasure?

SMALL: I was stationed in Agra with two Sikh troopers placed under my command, Mahomet Singh and Abdullah Khan. It was they who brought me into a plot with Dost Akbar. We made a pact and sealed it with the Sign of Four. You see, a Rajah in the Northern provinces sent half of his treasure in an iron box away when trouble broke out via a trusty servant disguised as a merchant. My associates and I murdered this servant and we took the treasure for our own. It was this murder that sent the four of us to Andaman. But we had secreted the treasure in a deserted part of the Agra fort.

HOLMES: The location of which you detailed on a map for Captain Morstan.

SMALL: Aye, he and Major Sholto had promised to get us away from Port Blair if we shared the treasure with them. I gave them the map and Sholto abandoned Morstan and left us there to rot.

HOLMES: So Morstan didn't betray you?

SMALL: He was an above board chap, all right in his way. He had a weak heart and spent a lot of time at the dispensary. I worked there when my leg was too bad for diggin'. It was Sholto that took the treasure and left the five of us at Andaman. If I had come upon Sholto alone, I would have ended him with a light heart.

HOLMES: Port Blair is where you met Tonga?

SMALL: As I said, I worked at the dispensary. One day a convict gang picked up a little Andaman Islander who was sick to death. He had gone to a lonely place to die. I took him in hand and after a couple of months I got him all right.

HOLMES: That would explain his devotion to you.

SMALL: Tonga was quite fond of me. He was a fine boatsman and owned a big roomy canoe of his own. It was then that I saw my chance of escape. Staunch and true, was little Tonga. No man ever had a more faithful mate.

HOLMES: I had hoped that Tonga has lost all his darts yet he managed to shoot one at us in the boat.

SMALL: He had lost them all, except the one which was in his blow-pipe at the time.

HOLMES: Ah, of course. I had not thought of that.

(Jones enters with Watson.)

JONES: Quite a family party. Well, I think we may all congratulate each other. Pity we didn't take the other alive, but there was no choice. I say Holmes, you must confess that you cut it rather fine. It was all we could do to overhaul her.

HOLMES: I certainly did not know that the Aurora was such a clipper.

JONES: Smith says she is one of the fastest launches on the river and if he had another man to help, we should never have caught her. He swears he knew nothing of the Norwood business.

SMALL: Neither he did. Not a word. We told him nothing and paid him well.

JONES: Well, if he did no wrong then we shall see no wrong comes to him. If we are quick in catching our men, we are not so quick in condemning them.

HOLMES: Well, Watson, how did Miss Morstan take to seeing the treasure?

WATSON: She's taking it rather well. *(Opening the box)* Being that it's all gone.

(Small leans back in his chair and laughs deeply)

JONES: This is your doing Small.

SMALL: I have put it where you shall never lay hands on it. It is my treasure and if I can't have it then I'll take good care that no one else does. No living man has right to it unless it is three men in the Andaman convict barracks and myself. It's been the sign of four with us always. I did exactly as they would have had me do – throw the treasure in the Thames. You'll find the treasure where the key and little Tonga is.

JONES: You are deceiving us, Small. It would have been easier for you to have thrown the box and all.

SMALL: Easier for me to throw and easier for you to recover. The man that was clever enough to hunt me down is clever enough to pick an iron box from the bottom of the river.

JONES: This is a very serious matter, Small. If you had helped justice, instead of thwarting it this way, you would have had a better chance at your trial.

SMALL: *(Passionately)* Justice! A pretty justice. Whose loot is this, if it is not ours? Look how I have earned it. Twenty long years in that swamp, all day at work under the mangrove-tree, all night chained up in the filthy convict huts, bitten with mosquitos and racked with fever. That was how I earned the Agra treasure and you talk to me of justice.

JONES: Well, Holmes, if you have had your questions answered we shall be going.

HOLMES: Every bit satisfied.

JONES: Good night gentlemen, both. You first Small.

(Jones, Small and Murcher exit.)

WATSON: Well, and there is the end of our little drama. I fear that it may be the first and last investigation in which I shall have the chance of studying your methods.

HOLMES: What do you mean?

WATSON: Miss Morstan has done me the honor to accept me as a husband in prospective.

HOLMES: *(Groaning)* I feared as much. I really cannot congratulate you.

WATSON: I'm a little hurt. Have you any reason to be dissatisfied with my choice?

HOLMES: Not at all. I think she is one of the most charming young ladies I ever met and might have been most useful in such work as we have been doing. She had a decided genius that way – witness the way she preserved the Agra plan from all the other papers of her father. But love is an emotional thing and whatever is emotional is opposed to that true cold reason which I place above all things. I should never marry myself, lest I bias my judgment.

WATSON: I trust that my judgment may survive the ordeal. But you look weary.

HOLMES: Yes, the reaction is already upon me. I shall be as limp as a rag for a week.

WATSON: Strange how terms of what in another man I should call laziness alternates with your fits of splendid energy and vigor.

HOLMES: Yes, there is the makings in me of a very fine loafer. Well, at least Jones finally has the right man.

WATSON: Holmes, your merits should be publicly recognized. It will not do for you to let Scotland Yard take all the credit for your accomplishments. You should publish an account of the case. If you won't, I will for you.

HOLMES: Do what you like, Doctor.

WATSON: I believe I will. Still, the division seems rather unfair. You have done all the work in this business. I get a wife out of it, Jones gets the credit, pray what remains for you?

HOLMES: For me, my dear Doctor Watson, there is always the next case.

END OF ACT 2

FIN

Appendices

Appendix 1 – Holmes' Chemical Experiment

We achieved the desired reaction for Holmes' chemical experiment using only vinegar and cabbage.

Boil shredded red cabbage leaves for 30 minutes and let cool. You will get a deep purple liquid that reacts to bases and acids. Preset the chemistry set with several test tubes containing the cabbage juice.

On the chemistry cart, set a wide mouthed container with a liter or so of white vinegar. Holmes will pretend to prick Watson's finger and place the blood in the vinegar. He tells the audience that it is water.

Holmes will then pour some of the vinegar into a beaker and then dump one of the test tubes of cabbage juice into the vinegar. The deep purple liquid will turn red when it reacts with the acid in the vinegar.

Appendix 2 – Props

- Act 1 Scene 1
  - Watson
    - Newspaper
  - Waiter
    - Menus
    - Serving Tray
    - Wine Bottles
    - Glasses
- Act 1 Scene 2
  - Holmes
    - Chemical Equipment
- Act 1 Scene 3
  - Holmes
    - Papers for Lestrade
    - Coins
    - Violin
    - Magnifying Glass
    - Pipe
    - Matches
    - Paper
    - Pencil/Pen
  - Watson
    - Watch
    - Victorian Magazine (Illustrated London News)
    - Handkerchief
  - Mary
    - Handbag
    - Letter and envelope
    - Address Labels from pearl boxes
    - Six large pearls

- Mrs. Hudson
  - Mary's calling card
  - Tray
- Act 1 Scene 4
  - Paperboy
    - Papers (London Times)
  - Mary
    - Agra Treasure Map
- Act 1 Scene 5
  - Thaddeus
    - Hookah
  - Watson
    - Stethoscope
- Act 1 Scene 7
  - Mrs. Bernstone
    - Lantern
  - Holmes
    - Lock-picking tools
    - Magnifying Glass
    - Matches
  - Bartholomew
    - Sign of Four Card
    - Blanket over back of chair
  - Watson
    - Handkerchief
  - Murcher
    - Lantern
- Act 2 Scene 1
  - Watson
    - Handkerchief
- Act 2 Scene 2
  - Holmes
    - Pipe
    - Handkerchief
  - Wiggins
    - Pouch with Poison Darts

- Act 2 Scene 3
  - Wiggins
    - Dog leash
  - Holmes
    - Coins
- Act 2 Scene 4
  - Mrs. Smith
    - Washcloth
  - Holmes
    - Coins
- Act 2 Scene 5
  - Holmes
    - Newspaper (London Times)
    - Tray with tea set
- Act 2 Scene 7
  - Watson
    - Cigars (pre-set)
    - Glasses (pre-set)
    - Alcohol Bottles (pre-set)
  - Jones
    - Telegram from Holmes
  - Holmes
    - Beard and Wig disguise
    - Oak Cudgel used as cane
- Act 2 Scene 8
  - Murcher
    - Green Lantern (pre-set)
    - Treasure Chest containing coal (pre-set)
  - Holmes
    - Pistol
    - Spyglass or binoculars
  - Watson
    - Pistol
  - Small
    - Wooden Crutch

- Smith
  - Yellow Lantern
- Act 2 Scene 9
  - Murcher
    - Treasure Chest
  - Small
    - Manacles
  - Holmes
    - Pipe
    - Matches

About The Author

Eric J. McAnallen is no stranger to the theatre having appeared in over 35 productions on Western PA Stages since 1984 when, as a sophomore in high school, he walked into the Senior Class Musical auditions and landed a principal role.

Eric earned a BA in Creative Writing from Carnegie Mellon University and was the winner of the Premier Performances Playwriting Award while studying Education at Duquesne University.

He is a native of Ellwood City, PA where he lives with his wife, Misa, his dog, Maximus, and a plethora of fish named Steve. Eric dreamed of being a well-known writer but life got in the way and today he is a professional IT Guru and his own webmaster.

Eric is a member of the Dramatists Guild of America and writes plays in his spare time.